AMULETS, TALISMANS & MAGICAL JEWELRY

AMULETS

TALISMANS

&

MAGICAL

JEWELRY

A Way to the Unseen,

Ever-Present, Almighty God

BARBARA BLACK KOLTUV, PH.D

NICOLAS-HAYS, INC.
Berwick, Maine

First published in 2005 by
Nicolas-Hays, Inc.
P. O. Box 1126
Berwick, ME 03901-1126
www.nicolashays.com

Distributed to the trade by
Red Wheel/Weiser, LLC
P. O. Box 612
York Beach, ME 03910-0612
www.redwheelweiser.com

Library of Congress Cataloging-in-Publication Data available on request.
Cover and text design by Kathryn Sky-Peck
Typeset in Dante
KT
PRINTED AND BOUND IN CHINA

10	09	08	07	06	05
6	5	4	3	2	1

The paper used in this publication meets the minimum requirements of the
American National Standard for Information Sciences—Permanence of Paper for
Printed Library Materials Z39.48–1992 (R1997).

CONTENTS

LIST OF ILLUSTRATIONS

ACKNOWLEDGMENTS

I acknowledge the many collectors and sellers of amulets, talismans, and magical jewelry in Jerusalem, New York, London, Morocco, Istanbul, and all the other places in the world where I've found them. Amulet collectors often seem to collect stories as well as amulets. I am as grateful to them for the stories as I am for the magical objects. I most especially thank Jack Haliveh, Ziad Kwas, Maher Natsheh, and Tammy and Sarah Einstein. They have taught me all kinds of things about amulets, talismans, and magical jewelry. I gratefully thank them for their generosity.

Rachel Elior, of Hebrew University in Jerusalem, lectures and teaches all over the world and writes about mystical thought, theosophy, imagination, and creativity in Jewish mystical literature from antiquity to Hasidism. She offered unstinting help in deciphering and translating some of the amulets. Her worksheets 1 and 2 for the *shiviti* amulet are shown in this book on pages 85–86. She also drew my attention to the distinction between mystical and magical language, and told me that the magical Samaritan letters shown in *Sefer Raziel* are called angel letters, or eyeglass letters. Professor Elior is an overflowingly generous teacher and friend.

Zipporah Sibahi Greenfield of Ein Kerem, Jerusalem, was born in Yemen. She taught me about my first Yemenite prayer case and generously shared her rich and original research on the silver jewelry and the wedding dress of the

Jewish women of Maswar, Yemen. Her research provides a rare and authentic insight into Jewish Yemenite amulets.

Ran Oron, sculptor, architect, and mystic, offered insights into the world of angels and translated the magical objects from the tomb of Rabbi Simeon bar Yohai.

Charlie Roth, Hasid extraordinaire, patiently and generously helped translate the amulets from the *Sefer Raziel* and has been a wonderful Torah learning partner for many years.

Gioia Timpanelli, storyteller and author, sister in spirit, and dear friend, intuitively found a copy of the rare *Sefer Raziel*, written in Hebrew, at the Woodstock Library sale. She gave it to me years ago, when I could barely read Hebrew—except for the title, which I recognized as a gem, even then.

I am grateful to my computer guru Joel Black who generously supported, trained, and taught me all I know about the computer. He also found this jewel of a laptop, a Libretto, or small book, which small as it is came with a *dybbuk* in it that grabbed hold of me and made me write this book. Joel also took many of the photographs of amulets and jewelry that appear in the book.

Both last and first I thank my mother, Anne Lautenschlager Black, who loved jewelry and took me to the "exchange" on Canal Street and introduced me to all the treasures there and let me choose my own magical jewelry when I was very young.

—BBK

PART ONE

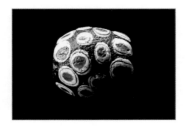

We have fallen upon hard times. We are lost, beset, alone, and afraid. We need help. The problems seem so overwhelming and insoluble that we look to God. Amulets, talismans, and magical jewelry provide a beautiful, tangible bridge between us and the unseen, ever-present God. They are prayers we can hold in our hands; something to hold onto when we seek help and protection from above.

First-Hand Faith

From earliest times, human beings have felt the need to concretize their connection with their God. There are rock paintings and stelae that speak to this need, many dating back thirty thousand years. These huge stelae were the Gods at that time; they were worshipped and feared. Even then, with these visually present and powerful Gods, and well-established forms and rituals for propitiating the Gods, people needed a personal way of connecting to the divine. Small personal amulets and talismans have been found in archeological digs all over the world, dating back thousands of years. Some are written or scratched on rock or metal, and some are simply pierced stones or beads.

Figure 1. A cache of ancient stone amulets with prayers inscribed on them from 8th-7th century B.C.E.

At first the Gods ruled with fear. Human beings were sacrificed to appease them, but then came a change: The entire Old Testament chronicles the emergence of a new way of consciousness. It tells of the One God who is the Creator of All, a God who creates man with free will and in God's own image. The stories of the Old Testament tell of a continual process of separation and individuation as human beings veer between the old way of fear and appeasement, and the new way of individual responsibility and choice.

The unseen, all-powerful monotheistic God of the Old Testament requires us to make our own choices based on a careful understanding of our own experience. In the face of the difficult task of becoming conscious and individuated, the human need for something tangible to hang onto (or to literally hang on oneself) persists. Amulets, talismans, and magical jewelry continue to be a vital connection between human beings and God.

The Old Testament tells of what has happened, is happening, and will continue to happen. My book shows how amulets, talismans, and magical jewelry are really prayers that provide a way for people to connect to the unseen, ever-present, almighty God. These treasured objects are a bridge between heaven and earth and something to hold on to.

No Idols, No Other Gods

And God spoke all these words to say:

> *I am the Lord your God who brought you out from the land of Egypt, from*
> *   the house of slavery.*
> *You shall have no other Gods before me.*
> *You shall not make for yourself an idol in the form of anything in heaven*
> *above or on the earth beneath or in the waters below. (Exodus 20:1–5)*

The second commandment of the Old Testament specifically forbids making an idol to represent God. However, human beings have always needed a direct and personal connection to the divine, and a way is provided in Exodus 25:8 when God says, *make me a sanctuary, that I may dwell among you.*

God goes on to instruct the people to make a tabernacle consisting of a chest overlaid with pure gold, with golden rings attached to it. He tells them to put poles of acacia wood overlaid with pure gold through the rings so the chest can be carried along as the children of Israel journey through the wilderness. The poles must remain in the rings of the chest and are not to be removed. (Exodus 25:10–16) Thus the Holy Ark is always ready to travel with the people as they move through the wilderness. The Ark is an amulet. It is tribal, and not yet personal, but it is present and not an idol or a God.

God tells the children of Israel to put into the Ark the testimony that he will give them. They are to make a cover for the Ark of pure gold and to make two cherubim of hammered gold, and to place them at each end of the cover. The cherubim must have their wings spread so that they surround the cover of the ark. God continues, telling Moses to instruct the children of Israel:

> *Place the cover on top of the ark of the Testimony onto the top and into the*
> *ark put the Testimony which I will give to you. There I will meet with you*

and I will tell to you from above the cover and from between the two cheru-
bim over the ark of the Testimony all that I command to you sons of Israel.
(Exodus 25:21–23)

So, unseen and surrounded by the wings of the cherubim, God came to dwell among the people as a divine presence called the *Shekhina*, a word from the Hebrew meaning "to dwell." Later as they stood at the base of Mount Sinai, Moses told the people:

Hear, O Israel: The Lord our God, the Lord is one.
Love the Lord your God with all your heart and with all your soul and with
all your strength. These commandments that I am giving you today must be
upon your heart. Impress them upon your children and talk about them
when you sit in your house and when you walk on the road, when you lie
down and when you get up. Tie them as signs on your hands and they must
be as frontlets between your eyes. Write them on the doorframes of your
house and on your gates. (Deuteronomy 6:4–10)

The injunction to keep the words of the Lord upon your heart—and to tie them as symbols on your hands, bind them on your foreheads, and to write them on the doorpost and gates of your house—seems to give permission—even to demand–that people carry and surround themselves with a concrete connection to the one unseen, ever-present God. Thus, the encased prayer became an approved amulet that offered a concrete and real connection to God.

The intimate relationship between God and man goes even further:

The Lord said to Moses, "Consecrate to me every firstborn male. The first off-
spring of a womb among the children of Israel belongs to me whether man or

animal." Then Moses said to the people, *"Commemorate this day, the day you came out of Egypt, out of the land of slavery, because the Lord brought you out of it with a mighty hand...."* (Exodus 13:1–4)

In another personal instruction God says:

> *For seven days eat bread made without yeast and on the seventh day hold a festival to the Lord. Eat only unleavened bread for those seven days; nothing with yeast in it is to be seen among you, nor shall any yeast be seen anywhere within your borders.*
>
> *On that day tell your son, "I do this because of what the Lord did for me when I came out of Egypt." And it will be for you like a sign on your hand and as a reminder between your eyes she must be, the law of the Lord in your mouth, for with a mighty hand the Lord brought you out of Egypt. And you must keep this ordinance at her time, from all the days to all the days.* (Exodus 13:6–11)

Figure 2. *Tie them as signs on your hands and they must be as frontlets between your eyes ...* A religious Jew with the phylacteries, or small boxes containing prayers, tied as frontlets between his eyes, and wrapped around his arm and hand.

Remembering the connection between human beings and God is made concrete in terms of what comes from the body and issues from the womb, what goes into the body through the mouth, what is said by the mouth, what is worn on the hand, and the forehead, and body, and what is written on the doorframes and gates of one's house that physically surrounds the body. What is thought in heart and mind, and when and how a festival of remembrance is celebrated, also connects us with God. All these stories, experiences, rememberings, and actions connect a person to the unseen, ever-present, almighty God.

AMULETS: NEARER TO GOD

An amulet is anything worn as a charm against evil, disease, witchcraft, and misfortune. The word *amulet* can be derived either from the Arabic word *hamalat*, meaning "to hang," or from the Hebrew word *kame'a*, which has the root meaning "to bind." Hanging, or binding, or wearing an amulet upon oneself protects the wearer. The word "amulet" may also be derived from the Latin word *amuletum*, from the verb *amdiri,* meaning "to remove or drive away." The Ark of the Covenant with its gold rings was hung permanently on the golden staves so the children of Israel could, at any and all times, carry it with them in their wanderings. Thus, it was a permanent protective amulet for the entire community.

Similarly, the modern translation of *tefillin* also implies that they are used for protection and for warding off of danger. The *totophot*, or bands to be worn on one's hand and on the forehead, are called *tefillin* or phylacteries. They are prayers written on parchment or on paper and encased in leather boxes. Leather straps are attached and the prayer cases are bound to the forehead and the arms. There is a ritual prayer and pattern for wrapping the leather straps on the arms and forehead and a special time and order for the daily ritual of putting on *tefillin*.

Figure 3. An old-fashioned *mezuzah* from Palestine.

The prayer that is fixed to the doorpost and gates of a house is called a *mezuzah,* from the Hebrew word for "gatepost." It consists of the prayer that begins:

> *Hear, O Israel: The Lord our God, the Lord is one. Love the Lord your God with all your heart and with all your soul and with all your strength . . . And ends with . . . Tie them as a sign upon your hand, and they must be as frontlets between your eyes. Write them on the doorframes of your house and on your gates.* (Deuteronomy 6:4–10)

It includes also:

> *So it will be if you obey my commands that I am giving you today to love the Lord your God, and to serve him with all your heart and with all your soul, then I will give the rain for your land in its season, the early rain and the later rain, so you may gather your grain and your new wine and your oil.*
>
> *And I will give grass in your fields for your cattle, and you will eat and you will be satisfied. Take heed lest your heart be enticed and you turn aside and serve other gods and worship them; and then the anger of the Lord will be kindled against you, and he will shut up the heavens that there will be no rain, and that the land will yield not her fruit, and you will perish quickly from off the good land which the Lord gave you.*

And the instructions:

Fix these words of mine in your heart and in your soul; and tie them as a sign upon your hand, and they must be as frontlets (totophot) *between your eyes. Teach them to your children, talking of them when you sit in your house, and when you walk on the way, and when you lie down, and when you rise. Write them upon the doorframes* (mezuzot) *of your house and upon your gates, so that your days and the days of your children may be many in the land which the Lord swore to your fathers to give them, as the days of the heavens above the earth.* (Deuteronomy 11:13–22)

The prayer is written on parchment or on paper and placed in a metal, wood, or ceramic case and affixed to the doorframe and gates of a house. Some homes have a mezuzah on the doorframe to each room. One is supposed to kiss it upon entering and leaving the room or house, in remembrance of God's commandment.

These objects— *mezuzot* and *tefillin*—may not ordinarily be thought of as amulets, but that is what they are. Amulets protect by making us re-member and make concrete our connection to God. The *mezuzah* on the gate and doorpost protects the person who loves and remembers God as he passes into the house. It also protects those inside from danger as it did on the first night of Passover when God told the Hebrews to put a sign on their doorposts so that the angel of death would pass over their houses and their firstborn sons would be protected, while the firstborn sons of the Egyptians with no sign for protection on their doorposts would be killed. (Exodus 12:7, 12–14)

Some amulets are called *segul* from a very ancient, unused Hebrew root meaning "shut up." The word *segul* is used in the Old Testament to describe the people of Israel as a valued property, a peculiar treasure which God has taken to Himself (Deuteronomy 7:6) and as a treasure of kings in Ecclesiastes (2:8).

For thou art an holy people unto the LORD thy God: the LORD thy God hath chosen thee to be a special people unto himself, above all people that are upon the face of the earth. The LORD did not set his love upon you, nor choose you, because ye were more in number than any people; for ye were the fewest of all people: But because the LORD loved you.
(Deuteronomy 7:6–8)

If the people of Israel are a treasure of God, chosen with love, and the amulet is a *segul* for protection from harm, one can see that the amulet is a bridge of love between human beings and God.

A dream, too, can have the power of an amulet. In the place he called Beit El, or "house of God," Jacob dreamt:

Figure 4. A laminated amulet showing a picture of the Rabbi Yosef Chaim on the front.

Behold—a ladder resting on earth with its top reaching to the heavens. And behold—angels of God, ascending ones and descending ones on it. And behold—the Lord standing above him said: I am the Lord, God of Abraham your father and God of Isaac. The land that you are lying upon I will give to you and to your descendants. Your descendants will be like dust of the earth and you will spread to west and to east and to north and to south. And they will be blessed through you, all the peoples of the earth, through offspring of you. And behold—I am with you and I will guard you

*in anywhere you go and I will bring you back to this land. Indeed I will not
leave you until I do what I said to you.* (Genesis 28:12–16)

*When Jacob awoke from his sleep he said, "Surely there is God in this place
and I knew it not."* (Genesis 28:17)

Jacob's dream occurs early in Genesis and clarifies the relationship between
the unseen God of the Hebrews and the embodied idols of the gods of the
surrounding people. Here in *Beresheit*, or the book of creation, Jacob dreams of angels as messengers ascending and descending between earth and heaven, and between man and God. In the dream Jacob hears God's promise to be with him and to guard him and to bring him back to the land he has promised to him. God seems to be saying that he needs to be with Jacob as people often feel that they need to be with God.

Later, when

*Jacob was alone by himself, a man— he wrestled
with him until the dawn came up. When the man
saw that he could not overpower him, he touched
the socket of his hip so that Jacob's hip was
wrenched as he wrestled with the man. Then the
man said, "Let me go, for the dawn comes." But
Jacob said, "I will not let you go unless you bless
me." And he said to him, "What is your name?"
And he answered, "Jacob." And the man said,*

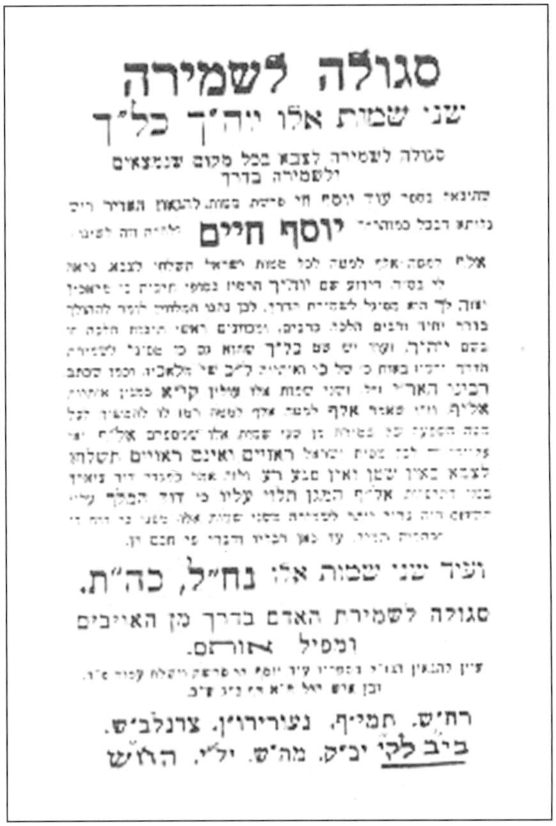

Figure 5. On the other side of Rabbi Yosef Chaim is a *segul* for
the protection of people who are sent to the army.

"You will not be called Jacob any longer, but your name is now Israel for you
struggled with God and with men and you have overcome.
(Genesis 32:25–28)

So Jacob called the name of the place Peniel, "For I saw God face to face
and yet my life was spared." The sun rose above him just as he crossed over
from Peniel and he was limping because of his hip . . . (Genesis 32:30–32)

The name of the place is Peniel, from the word *peh,* meaning "mouth" and "face," and *El,* meaning "God." Jacob was mouth to mouth and face to face with God as they wrestled.

The name Jacob, *Ya'akov,* is derived from *ekev,* or "heel," because Jacob was born clutching at the heel of his twin brother Esau. Jacob is changed forever from the lowest most humble part, *ekev* or heel, the part of the body that is closest to the ground and touches the ground first as human beings walk upon earth, to Israel, which means "struggles with God." In the dream of wrestling with the angel of God, the angel smites Jacob on the hip and when he wakes, Jacob limps. This dream is so vivid that we recognize it as what we now call a waking dream. It has a reality so strong that it changes the dreamer forever. The words and images heard and seen in a dream can have a powerful effect when they are attended to. They are so direct and meaningful that people feel that they are given by a more creative and supernal consciousness than their own waking ego. Indeed, the Talmud states that a dream uninterpreted is like an unopened letter. A dream owned, held on to, and interpreted is a powerful protective healing amulet.

TALISMANS: BEADS AND PRAYER

The strange word *talisman* is of uncertain origin. It is a name formerly attributed to a Turkish *mullah* educated in divinity and law, and sometimes to a lower priest of Islam, a *muezzin*. It sounds very like the Hebrew word *tallis,* the prayer shawl that religious men wrap themselves in while praying. The word *talisman* comes from the Arabic word *talisam,* meaning "to make marks like a magician." *Talisam* in turn comes from the Greek word *telsam,* meaning "to initiate by incantation."

While there is only one God for the Children of Israel, there are 613 commandments. In Numbers 15:37–41 they are instructed to look upon the *tallis,* or prayer shawl, which must have four tassels made of blue and white silk, and remember all 613 commandments. Thus, the commandments are remembered and counted by the prayer shawl having 600 fringes, eight strings, and five knots. Human beings remember God and meditate on his miracles and commandments using concrete objects and rituals. The food we eat and drink when blessed or when its source is remembered becomes a talisman. Even the word re-membering has a talismanic meaning. To member something means to bring together in a particular intentional way. This is the function of a talisman and prayer.

Talismans need not have letters or words although many do, while amulets always bear letters or words. Talismans often have a ritual counting and/or chanting form. Prayers counted out on beads are common to Hindus, Buddhists, and Catholics. Muslims, like Jews have only one God, Allah, but He is known by many names reflecting his attributes. Prayer beads are used to count out His names as prayers. Similarly, Rabbi Nachman of Bratzlev, in his classic work on meditation, *Outpouring of the Soul*, suggests that chanting the name of God over and over again is a simple and effective way to connect with God directly.

From the beginning, life is entombed within the rhythmic sound of pulse and heartbeat. One Yeshivah student, while observing the sea of praying moving bodies around him, said that, although the Torah law does not require constant movement while praying, everyone does do it, as the flame of a candle does. The safe reassurance of this cadence is the basis for chanting and counting prayers. One can easily imagine the development of a system of piling stones, praying, and moving a stone, praying, and moving another stone, and so on, and so on. From this stationary act followed the process of drilling a hole through each stone, and suspending them on a string or thong so that they could easily be moved while prayers were said and counted. So there were prayer beads. The word *bead* is from the old English word *bede*, and means "prayer" or "devotion."

Figure 6. Sufi sheikh with amber prayer beads.

Figure 7. Islamic prayer beads made from pearls, glass, coral inlaid with silver, and amber.

The rosary is a set of prayer beads well-known to the Christian world. Many faiths and cultures have their own form of prayer beads. Muslims, for example, use strands of 33, 66, or 99 beads with separators between each group of 11 beads on the 33 bead sets, and between each group of 33 beads on the 99 bead sets of prayer beads. The 99 beads represent the 99 names of the one God,

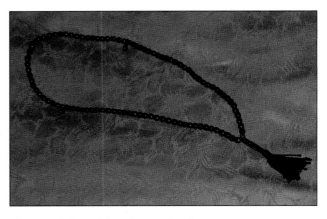

Figure 8. Black coral (*yussr*) prayer beads.

Allah. Muslim prayer beads have a long minaret shaped piece sometimes called the *aleph* because it represents the entrance into the circle of prayer.

When Fatima, the beloved daughter of the Prophet Muhammad, asked her father for a maid to help her, he taught her the special prayer to use with the beads: On the first 33 beads she was to say, *Allah ahkbar*, God is great, 33 times, and on the second group of 33 beads she should say, *La illaha illa'lla*, there is no God but God, and on the last 33 beads she should say, *Subhan'u'Allah*, God is the all Splendorous. These prayers are called "Fatima's broom," because they brought her all the help she needed.

The Muslims in the Old City of Jerusalem call their beads a *Subha*, from the prayer *Subhan'u'Allah*, praising God as All Splendor. Sometimes the beads are called a *misbaha*, which means recitation. Persian and Lebanese

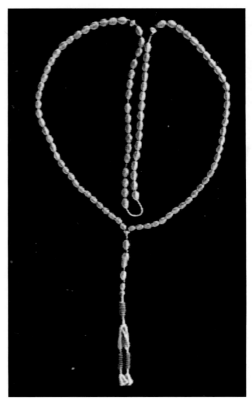

Figure 9. Muslim prayer beads from Turkey, and also used in Afghanistan, made from a rare green stone called *shah magsoud*.

Figure 10. A Naqshabandi sheikh with his prayer beads.

6.
Meditate on 3rd
Mystery, saying
the "Our Father,"
ten "Hail Marys"
and the "Glory Be."

7.
Meditate on 4th
Mystery, saying
the "Our Father,"
ten "Hail Marys"
and the "Glory Be."

5.
Meditate on 2nd
Mystery, saying
the "Our Father,"
ten "Hail Marys"
and the "Glory Be."

8.
Meditate on 5th
Mystery, saying
the "Our Father,"
ten "Hail Marys"
and the "Glory Be."

4.
Meditate on 1st Mystery,
saying the "Our Father,"
ten "Hail Marys" and
the "Glory Be."

9.
Concluding prayers,
"Hail Holy Queen"
and "Let Us Pray:
O God, whose only
begotten Son, etc."

3.
Say three "Hail Marys"
and the "Glory Be."

2.
Say the "Our Father."

1.
Make the Sign of the Cross,
say the Apostles' Creed.

Figure 11. A diagram of the rosary suggesting the prayers and meditations that form the rose garden of Mary.

Sufis call it a *tasbeh*, but all Muslims use the beads as a talisman for re-membering and experiencing God's greatness and manifold presence.

Muslim prayer beads are made of *anbar*, or amber, or of *yussr*, which is black coral sometimes inlaid with silver or mother-of-pearl, olive wood, plastic, bone, agate, glass, horn, ivory, pearl, and many other materials both precious and common. One revered Sufi master used a wonderful *tasbeh*, or set of wooden beads, with a large safety pin as an *aleph*. Customarily there is a tassel or three chains with balls on the ends of them at the bottom of the *aleph*. This is said to ward off the evil eye. One can imagine the flared points of the tassel or the three-part charm poking out the evil eye.

The Crusaders may have carried the practice of counting prayers on beads back to Western Europe from the East. However, according to Christian tradition the rosary has been in use all through the centuries from the time of the apostles until the present. Irish monks in the Dark Ages around A.D. 800 counted prayers by reciting the one hundred and fifty psalms of David. People who could not read or memorize such long passages of scripture began saying one hundred and fifty Paternoster, or Our Father, prayers using one hundred and fifty pebbles to keep count. This practice evolved into strings of one hundred and fifty knots, and then into strings of fifty beads. A rosary today has fifty beads arranged in five decades or sets of

Figure 12. Rose-scented rosary beads from Maggigore where Mary has appeared to the faithful in recent times.

ten beads. While saying the prayers, it is customary to meditate on the mysteries of the life of Jesus from his birth to his resurrection.

In A.D. 1214, Holy Mother Church received the rosary in its present form. It was given to the Church by Saint Dominic, who received it from the Blessed Virgin. The rosary takes its name from the rose, which in medieval times was seen as a symbol of life eternal. Mary, the first to be redeemed by Christ, has been called the *Rosa Mystica*, or the Mystical Rose.

Figure 13. *Tallit* showing details of the knots. Before donning his *tallis*, a man must untangle the fringes and examine them carefully to ensure that none of the strings have been torn. It is especially important to check the places where the strings are looped through the holes in the corners of the garment before they are knotted. If the *tzitzis* is torn there, the garment is not kosher or valid. (Photograph by Matthew Septimus)

Make tzitzit or tassels on the corners of your garment . . .
(Deuteronomy 22:12)

People of all religions chant prayers and make rhythmic movements while praying. The body is counting the cadence of prayers and both membering and re-membering the sound and words of the prayer. Buddhists, Muslims, and Catholics use prayer beads to count out the prayers. The Jews, while not using beads for prayer, do however, wear a ritual garment with *tzitzit,* or tassels, at the corners. These *tzitzit* are made by making a knot in the fringes at the corners of the garment. These knots are a form of bead and can be used for counting prayers. The very sound of the word *tzitzit* connotes the hard fact of a bead or prayer.

People often pray wrapped in a prayer shawl. The Talmud says that there are two hundred and forty eight important organs in the human body and the same number of positive commandments. It says there are three hundred and sixty five sinews and the same number of negative commandments. Therefore the Jewish sages conclude, man was created in order to perform God's will. The total number of organs and sinews in man, and the total number of divine commandments are each six hundred and thirteen, a number symbolized by the commandment of *tzitzis.* The sum of the mystical numbers equivalent to the letters that form the word *tzitzis* is six hundred. The five knots and eight threads of each fringe make up the other thirteen. Thus, by wrapping one's body in a *tallis* one dedicates himself totally to serving God. Because the *tallis* itself symbolizes the splendor of God's commandments, one feels cloaked in light by a garment that stretches out the heavens like a curtain, and offers protection, elevation, and illumination.

There are four separate passages in the Old testament commanding one to put on phylacteries. These passages are written on parchment and placed in the leather *totophot* or *tefillin.* Many people state that their intention in donning *tefillin* is "For the sake of the unification of The Holy One, blessed is He, and His Presence, in fear and in love, to unify his name." The *tefillin* that are wrapped around the arm relates to God's strength and the person's resolve to submit his heart and power to God. A right-handed person places the *tefillin* on his left arm, because it is the weaker one, and a left-handed person puts it on his right arm. The *tefillin* worn on the head represents one's resolve to dedicate the seat of one's intellect to God. The leather straps are wrapped seven times around one's arm, and around the middle finger and hand while saying, "I will betroth you to Me forever, and I will betroth you to Me with righteousness, justice, kindness, and mercy. I will betroth you to me with fidelity, and you shall know God." One then recites the four passages from scripture contained in the prayer boxes.

The tradition of chanting prayers among all the various communities of Jewish people has at its root the same talismanic rhythmic counting, or initiation by incantation. The chanting itself induces a meditative, reflective, receptive state and a person enters the circle of prayer. There is also the tradition of covering one's head, and wrapping oneself completely in a *tallis* or prayer shawl to heighten the experience of oneness with God through prayer. In this sense the *tallis* is also a talisman. A person becomes one with his inner sense of the divine source. Healing occurs in this state. Answers become clear. There is deep comfort and well-being and joy. The Chassids call this experience *d'vekut*, or "cleaving to God," and becoming one with God.

While the Israelites wandered in the wilderness, the One Unseen God continued to speak to Moses and tell him what to teach the people about the new laws and the new way of living. God makes a distinction between someone who sins unintentionally and someone who sins defiantly. Clearly, the new monotheism requires a face-to-face wrestling, consciousness and participation, choice and personal responsibility.

While the sons and daughters of Israel were in the desert they found a man who was gathering wood on the day of the Sabbath. They brought him to Moses and to Aaron and to the whole of the assembly. They kept him in custody because it was not clear what should be done to him. Then said the Lord to Moses:

Die, the man must die. The whole assembly must stone him with stones out-
side the camp.

So they took him the whole of the assembly to outside of the camp and
they stoned him with the stones and he died just as the Lord commanded to
Moses. (Numbers 15: 32–37)

Immediately following this report the Bible says:

The Lord said to Moses, "Speak to the children of Israel. Say to them that
they must make tzitzit *or tassels on the corners of their garments. Through*
the generations of them they must put on the tassel at the corner a cord of
blue. It will be to you as a tzitzit *and you will see it and you will remember*
all the commands of the Lord, and you will obey them and not prostitute
yourselves and go after your hearts and your eyes. Then you will remember
and you will obey all of my commands and will be consecrated one to your
God. I am the Lord your God who brought you from the land of Egypt to be
for you as God. I am the Lord, God of you." (Numbers 15:37–41)

The clear statement here is that people need to be discriminating and responsible for their own choices. God says they have been chosen for a particular
type of new consciousness. He brought them out of Egypt, or *Mitzriyim*—the
narrow place, where they were slaves and had no personal responsibility—so
that He could be their God. The fringes on the four corners of the garment
symbolize their diverse choices, while the hard knots are like beads of consciousness making the people re-member both their own free will, and the
laws of the new way of the unseen ever-present God who needs to be remembered in the talisman of the knot, the bead, and the prayer.

Jewelry in itself has a certain magic—it connotes something more than mere apparel or adornment—and has a symbolic value. Jewelry shows wealth or power, and sometimes carries a ritual meaning.

When God instructs Moses about how to make the Ark of the Covenant, God also tells Moses to have an *ephod* and a breast piece made for Aaron, the high priest. Aaron is to wear this garment and this heavy piece of jewelry for his *k'vod,* or honor, and for his *tifferet*, a word that is hard to translate. *Tifferet* is more than "beauty"; it includes glory, and strength, and loving-kindness, as well.

And they shall make the ephod of gold, blue, purple and scarlet yarn, and fine twisted linen—the work being skilled. . . . (Exodus 28:6)

And you shall take two stones of onyx and engrave on them the names of the sons of Israel —six names on the one stone and the names of the six remaining ones on the other stone in order of their births. The work of the cutter of stone must be engraved as one engraves a seal. The two stones with the names of the sons of Israel: mount them in settings of gold filigree. Fasten the two stones on the shoulder pieces of the ephod as stones of remembrance for the sons of Israel. Aaron shall bear their names on his two shoulders before the Lord as a remembrance. Make filigrees of gold and two chains of pure gold braided. Make them like work of rope and attach the chains of rope to the settings.

Make a breast piece of judgment—of skilled work like the work of the ephod. Make it of gold, blue, purple and scarlet yarn, and of fine linen, twisted. Make it square. It shall be doubled—a span long and a span wide. Then mount on it settings for stones. Four rows for stones. In the first row

Figure 14. Statue of Aaron in garb of the high priest

there shall be a ruby, a topaz and a beryl; in the second row a turquoise, a sapphire and an emerald; in the third row a jacinth, an agate and an amethyst; in the fourth row a chrysolite, an onyx and a jasper. Mount them in gold filigree settings. There are to be twelve stones, one for each of the names of the sons of Israel, each engraved like a seal with the name of one of the twelve tribes. (Exodus 28:9–22)

Aaron will bear the names of the sons of Israel on the breast piece of judgment over his heart when he comes into the Holy Place. He does this as a continual remembrance before God.

And you shall put in the breast piece of judgment the Urim and the Thummim so they may be on the heart of Aaron when he comes before God. Aaron will bear the means of making judgments for the sons of Israel on his heart, before God, continually. (Exodus 28:29–31)

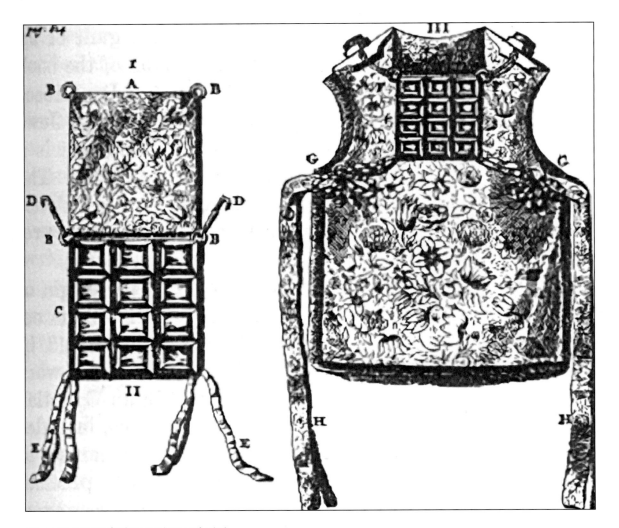

Figure 15. Pattern for breast piece and *ephod*.

The *ephod* is a garment that was worn under the breast piece and served to anchor it, and to enhance its magical and spiritual value. Both of the onyx stones at the shoulders had the names of the sons of Jacob incised on them for remembrance of the progenitors of the twelve tribes. Remembering the names and deeds of the sons who came before him helped Aaron carry out the responsibilities of his priestly office. Using the name of a person persists

Figure 16. Two views of the High Priest dressed in his magical garb, surrounded by inserts showing at top the materials used to make each part of his attire. There is the cochineal snail for blue dye, gold thread, linen, and a sheep for wool. The side inserts show the various pieces of the priest's apparel.

in amulet making even today. God has many names but is only one God. People have only one name, and in important matters are described as the son or daughter of someone so that there is no confusion as to which individual is meant. Each stone of the breast piece is carefully named and placed. Each stone has an individual meaning that is expressed in its placement and color, each stone represents the tribe of each son of Jacob.

The robe of the *ephod* itself is an amulet. Apparel dedicated to a particular role is really a double amulet. It protects the person who wears it from being overly identified with his role and losing himself, and it serves to carry some of the authority of the office. The robe of the *ephod* protected the high priest from being consumed by the needs of his people by marking his role. However, there is also danger from the inside. The high priest may fall into a dangerous identification with his role, and become inflated with the power that is truly God's. Therefore, the Bible gives careful instructions about construction and design of the high priest's garment:

> *And you shall make the robe of the ephod all of blue cloth. It shall have in it an opening for the head in the center. The edge of the opening shall have a woven work around it like the opening of a collar so that it will not tear.*
> (Exodus 28:31–33)

The strong woven binding around the neck opening accommodates the need to remove the garment when the high priest is not serving a priestly function.

The band around the neck which must not tear provides a boundary and a symbolic separation of mind and body that protects the high priest. Blue is the heavenly color used in the Middle East on doors and door frames, windows and window frames to fool the evil eye into believing that there is nothing but sky within a house, no human beings vulnerable to its evil intent.

> *You shall make on its hem pomegranates of blue and purple and scarlet stuff around its skirts, with bells of gold between them all around, a bell of gold and a pomegranate, a bell of gold and a pomegranate, on the hems of the robe all around. And it will be upon Aaron when he ministers, and its sound shall be heard when he goes into the holy place before the Lord, and when he comes out, lest he die.* (Exodus 28:33–36)

The pomegranates embroidered around the hem of the priest's garment are full of seeds. Pomegranates are used frequently in the Old Testament to connote a natural fecundity, a sense of the many potential choices, and a reminder that God is the source of everything. The bells are amulets to sound a warning and protect Aaron from the death he would certainly be dealt if he entered or departed the Holy of Holies improperly and without the appropriate preparation and consciousness.

> *You shall make a plate of pure gold and engrave upon it like the engraving on a signet: Holy to the Lord. You shall put upon it a thread of blue and it shall be upon the mitre, upon the forefront of the mitre it shall be. And it shall be upon Aaron's forehead . . .* (Exodus 28:36–39)

According to tradition, this plate was two fingers wide and extended across the entire forehead. The Hebrew word used here and throughout these instructions for "engrave" on the high priest's magical jewelry is *p'etach*. It means "develop." The same root, *peh, tav, chet,* is used for "open" and "key." Thus, by engraving the letters and words in this careful way, one opens the stone or metal in the form of a particular letter and word, and simultaneously, both open and develop the stone or metal amulet. There is magic and holiness inherent in this process.

The last and most mysterious element of these objects and garments of the high priest are the *Urim* and *Thummim*, which are to be used for decision making. The *ephod* was folded in half to form a secret pocket into which the *Urim* and *Thummim* were placed. This secret pocket lay close to Aaron's heart. At the ordination of Aaron and his sons, Moses placed the breast piece on Aaron and put the *Urim* and *Thummim* in the breast piece. (Leviticus 8:8)

The words *Urim* and *Thummim* mean literally "the lights" and "perfection." In times of doubt people consulted the *Urim* and *Thummim* for enlightenment and guidance. The exact procedure for consulting these oracles is never described. Nor were the objects themselves described. Rashi thought they were stone lots with words engraved on them. It is also possible that it was one object with "Urim" engraved on one side, and "Thummim" on the other. It seems likely the object or objects indicated the nature of the divine will by the way they fell. A distraught King Saul tried to find answers using the *Urim* and *Thummim*:

> *Therefore Saul said, "O Lord, God of Israel, why have you not answered your servant this day? If this guilt is in me or in Jonathan my son, O Lord, God of Israel, give Urim; but if this guilt is in your people Israel, give Thummim." And Jonathan and Saul were taken, but the people escaped.* (Samuel 14: 41–35)

And again, in dire straits:

When Saul saw the army of the Philistines, he was afraid, and his heart
trembled greatly. And when Saul inquired of the Lord, the Lord did not
answer him, either by dreams, or by Urim, or by prophets. Then Saul said
to his servants, "Seek out for me a woman who is a medium, that I may go
to her and inquire of her." And his servants said to him, "Behold, there is a
medium at Endor." (Samuel 28:5)

The *Urim* and *Thummim* together are a very special kind of amulet used as an
oracle. They belonged to the priestly class, and were used only by the priest.
When Moses blessed the tribes just before he died . . .

. . . of Levi he said, "Your Thummim, and your Urim belong to the man
you favored, whom you tested at Massah, you contended with him at the
waters of Mer'ibah. (Deuteronomy 33:7–10)

It is likely that when King Saul consulted the *Urim* and *Thummim* he did so by
asking Samuel the high priest at that time to read the oracle on his behalf.

When the Children of Israel returned from exile in Babylon no one was
sure of who the priests really were since they had intermarried, so the oracle
of the *Urim* and *Thummim* itself was used to determine who could use the
Urim and *Thummim*:

Also, of the sons of the priests:

. . . the sons of Habai'ah, the sons of Hakkoz, and the sons of Barzil'lai
(who had taken a wife from the daughters of Barzil'lai the Gileadite, and

was called by their name). These sought their registration among those enrolled in the genealogies, but they were not found there, and so they were excluded from the priesthood as unclean. (Ezra 2:61)

. . . the governor told them that they were not to partake of the most holy food, until a priest should appear wearing the Urim and Thummim.... (Ezra 2:63.25)

The *Urim* and *Thummim* are magical jewelry because possession of them is a sign of the priestly role. They function as protective amulets by protecting the priest who wears them, and as a prophetic device that helps him make decisions.

PART TWO

THE MIDDLE WORLD 5

According to the Talmud, as night drew near on the sixth day of creation, there was *la'asot*, or, "more to do," "something left to be done," "as yet unfinished." From this opening comes the *midrash*, or interpretation of *la'asot*—the last word of Genesis 2:3, that as twilight fell on the sixth day, God had created these spirits and had not yet had time to create their bodies. These unfinished elements are the spirits of evil, the *ruach ra'ah* that inhabit the middle world, that is, the place which is in-between heaven and earth. Because they have no bodies of their own, these spirits try to inhabit the bodies of humans and animals. Jewish *midrash* and folklore, too, understand Genesis 6:19 to mean that every living creature on Noah's ark included these evil spirits and demons.

Another version of how evil spirits came to inhabit the earth is found in the *Pseudepigrapha*, or *Apocrypha*. These are the writings of priests who were not in service at the Temple in Jerusalem, and writings that were left out of the Canon. There, a story only mentioned in Genesis is expanded upon.

> . . . .the sons of God saw that the daughters of man were beautiful and
> they took for them wives from any whom they chose . . . The Nephilim were
> on the earth in those days—and also after then—when the sons of God
> went to the daughters of Adam they bore to them—they —the heroes of

ever, men of the name . . . and the Lord saw how great the evil of man on the earth was, and every inclination of thought in his heart was only evil all of the day. (Genesis 6:1–6)

The offspring of this union are the evil spirits called *sheddim*. They are some of the evil spirits who inhabit the middle world seeking to invade and despoil human beings, and fill them with fear and dread.

On the day that Adam and Eve were banished from the Garden of Eden, *midrash* tells that Adam separated from his helpmeet Eve, feeling that she had led him astray. He sat alone, in despair, beside the river Gishon that flowed from Gan Eden, and prayed for help. Some say the angel Gabriel, the rescuer, appeared to him and gave him the book called the *Sefer Raziel*. Others say that the book was given to Adam by the angel Raziel itself. This small volume is the oldest source book for making amulets. The angel Raziel is believed to have been instructed in the tradition of Kabbalah directly by God. The Hebrew word *raz* means "secret," and the suffix *el* refers to God.

Amulets and talismans are used to keep evil spirits away and to protect people from them. Because everything was created *ex nihilo* by God, it is necessary, when dealing with the various evil spirits, to invoke the names of God and the names of the Angels to carry the message to God. Children often make up prayers or incantations to help keep the bad spirits away. Even before they can speak, you can hear babies humming, or see them rocking, or twirling their hair, or making certain incantations and gestures. A man of seventy years remembers imagining, when he was a boy, that the Lord's Prayer was a ladder of ascent to God. He thought that if he got it just right he would be safe. A woman remembers that, as a child, she tried to keep in the back of her mind a continuous image of trolley cars attached to each other, and attached to the sparking wire above, and to the iron tracks

Figure 17. The title page from *Sefer Raziel*.

beneath them. If she could keep this image moving—a vision of connection to the middle world and to what was above and to what was below—she felt safe. Both of these childhood images are reminiscent of Jacob's dream of the ascending and descending angels. Certain names of God must be used if one is to be safe from the evil spirits of the middle world, and there are particular angels needed in order to carry certain messages from man on earth to God in heaven. The Hebrew word for messenger and angel is the same: *malachim.*

The Evil Eye

A particular element of the middle world is the evil eye. It has existed since earliest times in every culture. Figure 18 is an ancient eye-bead from Phoenicia. The Phoenicians were seafarers, plying their trade all up and down the coasts of the Ancient World. Wherever they went, people believed that there was an evil eye, an evil intention sometimes attributed to a demonic force, and sometimes an attribute of a human being. Sometimes the evil intention was the result of an evil spirit entering into and possessing a human being. The evil eye can be warded off by a *beneficent* eye and also by a protective hand.

Figure 18. Phoenician eye-bead.

Even Rashi, a Talmudist and rationalist, has spoken about the evil eye, saying that a man would say that his beautiful baby is an "Ethiopian," which meant an ugly, dark, inferior being. By naming the beloved as ugly, the evil eye is thwarted in its destructive intention. Among some Jewish people, babies are not named for people who died young because of fear that the evil eye will strike again. Newborn children are called the *alte,* or "old ones"

Figure 19. A child's ankle bracelet with a blue button to protect the little girl who wears it from the evil eye.

to fool the evil spirits and protect against the evil eye seeing that there is human joy in the new life.

Figure 20. The wholesale market behind the Grand Bazaar in Istanbul, 1999. Thousands of glass eye-beads are sold as amulets for protection against the evil eye. (Photograph by Bryn Kelsey.)

Figure 21. This amulet was given to a Jewish woman when her first son was born. Her Iraqi mother-in-law had received the amulet from her own mother-in-law when her first son was born. The inner beads are blue faïence, covered and caged in 22 carat gold wire. They symbolize apples or pomegranates that are rich and fecund. The amulet has pink Jerusalem stones at either end and on the tiny *hamsa* dangling below. Sometimes blue stones are used instead of Jerusalem stone for added protection. (Photograph by Junenoire.)

Figure 22. A book containing the *noam*, or "sweetness" of the Chassidic Rebbe Eli Melech of Lezshinsk. It is an amulet for the protection of the *yeled*, or boy child, and the one who bears the child. The small book is to be placed under the pillow of the mother during childbirth. It promises to give her aid and reinforcement for an easy birth. The amulet on the back cover of the book is for protection against the child-killer Lilith.

Childbirth is a dangerous time for both the mother and the baby. Amulets are used to protect both the woman in labor and the newborn. A chalk circle is drawn around the bed of the woman in childbirth. An actual knife, or an amulet like the one shown in figure 66, is placed under the woman's pillow to cut the pain and protect her from the succubus and child-killer known as Lilith. Until the beginning of the twentieth century, an oil lamp called *ta'ara* was sometimes brought from a synagogue on the day before the circumcision ceremony. It was lit at the head of the baby's cradle to protect him from evil spirits. Sages sat in the room all night and read from the *Zohar,* or *Book of Splendor,* of the Kabbalists. This night was known as *Layl ha Ta'ara,* or the Night of the Ta'ara.

Figure 23. A bracelet with a protective glass eye-bead meant to protect a baby from the evil eye.

Among Jewish people there is an almost universal custom of prefacing the reply to a question about a baby's age, or well-being, or a compliment with the words, *"k'ain ayin ha-ra."* The phrase means, literally, "there is no evil eye." It is actually a verbal talisman meaning, "Please God, let there be no evil eye

Figure 24. Evil eye earrings and North African charms used by both Jews and Muslims to guard against the evil eye.

watching, here, now." Sometimes the protective gesture of spitting three times to the left and to the right is added to the talisman. Sometimes the gestures of a fist with the thumb inserted between the index and middle finger, or a fist with the index finger and pinkie extended, are used to poke out the evil eye. Fear of the evil eye extends so far back in time that this gesture is named for the ancient god Baal: the Horns of Baal. The point in the crescent

Figure 25. Elaborate fringes to poke out the evil eye, and woven designs symbolizing eyes, are used to protect these camels from the evil eye.

of the North African charms seen in figure 24 is another image for thwarting the evil eye.

Domestic animals, while not as precious as one's children, are important to a family's well-being, and thus vulnerable to the evil eye and in need of protective amulets. The crescent, or *saharon,* referred to in Judges 8:26 is an amulet tied to the necks of camels to protect them from the evil eye. The fringes still seen today in the Middle East adorning animals' saddlebags and packs in the Middle East are remnants of amulets and talismans used to poke out the evil eye.

The Old Testament abounds with references to both the benevolent eye and to the terrible, jealous evil eye. Here is a wonderful description of how God watches over the children of Israel, keeping an eagle eye upon them. They are called the "apple of His eye." The story of how God rescued Jacob is told in the Old Testament:

> *He found him in the land of the wilderness, and in barren and howling waste. He encircled him, he cared for him, he kept him as the apple of his eye. Like an eagle he stirs up his nest, he hovers over his young ones, he spreads his wings, he catches him, he carries him on his pinions. The Lord alone did lead him, and there was no foreign god with him.* (Deuteronomy 32:10–13)

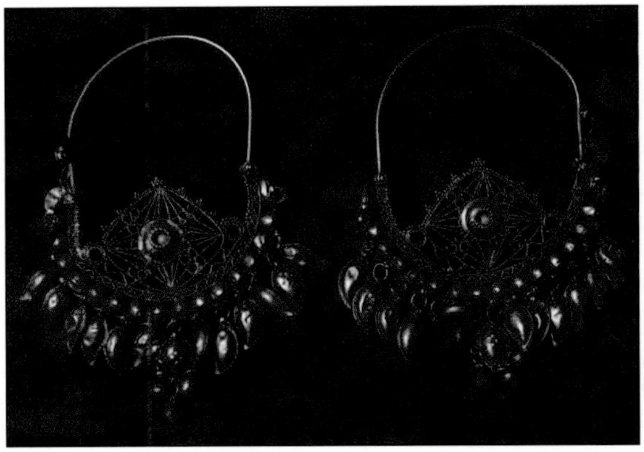

Figure 26. Gold earrings in the shape of eyes worn by women of Kurdistan. Both the shape of the earrings and the tiny blue stones are protection against the evil eye. The dangling comma-shaped gold pieces are stylized hearts used throughout the Middle East as amulets. (Photograph by Junenoire.)

Similarly, Proverbs 7:2 enjoins people to

> *. . . keep my commands and live, keep my teachings as the apple of your eye.*

God wants his commandments to be the apple of our eye. The Hebrew word *ishon,* which is translated as "apple," also means the "pupil" of the eye. In Arabic, the word for this benevolent eye is *bath ayin*, or "daughter of the eye." God wants his laws to be the central focus of our behavior. The magical forty-two letter name of God is based on a Sabbath prayer that begs God to keep the children of Israel as the apple of his eye. While the benevolent eye of God gives loving protection, His eye can also be full of jealous wrath:

> *They made him jealous with their foreign Gods; and angered him with their detestable idols.* (Deuteronomy 32:16–17)

> *By the sins they committed they stirred up his jealous anger more than their fathers had done.* (I Kings 14:22)

Counting or naming are experienced as making, having dominion over or creating. These are God's prerogatives and jealously guarded by the eye of God. When David in his pride took a census of his people God sent a plague which destroyed 70,000 of the 1,300,000 men of Israel and Judea. (2 Samuel 24:1–18)

Jealousy is a terrible issue for human beings as well as for God. It causes flashes of the evil eye:

> *Set me as a seal upon your heart, as a seal upon your arm; for love is strong as death, jealousy is cruel as the grave. Its flashes are flashes of fire, a mighty flame.* (Song of Songs 8:6–7)

The evil spirits that inhabit the middle world are often the projections of human beings. Those who either consciously or unconsciously intend evil toward others can express these feelings through their eyes. One might say that envy is a truer manifestation of the evil eye than jealousy. The intention of envy is to spoil what someone else has or feels, while jealousy merely covets what another has. Jealousy, consciously experienced, may engender competition or heroic action, but envy exudes a pernicious, spoiling energy. Paradoxically, both extreme unconsciousness and extreme consciousness heighten the power of the evil eye.

> *Anger is cruel and fury overwhelming; but who can stand before jealousy?* (Proverbs 27:4–5)

When the Philistines had been defeated, the women came out to greet the returning King Saul. The women danced and as they danced they sang:

> *Saul has slain his thousands and David his tens of thousands . . . Saul eyed David from that day forward.* (I Samuel 18:9–10)

Although the Hebrew word used here is *oyen*, or simply, "eyed," it is usually translated as "jealously eyed" so closely linked are the evil eye and jealousy and envy.

The evil eye can engender bad feeling within as well as for others, and the Torah warns of this:

Guard yourself so the wicked thing does not come to your heart to say "It is near the seventh year, the year of canceling debt" and she is your evil eye toward your needy brother, and you give him nothing, and he cries against you to the Lord and it will be sin in you. (Deuteronomy 15:9–10)

Psalm 141:4 is a talisman against various bodily openings being invaded by, or being the source for, the evil spirits of jealous envy that would then cause a person to cast an evil eye upon someone else. Instead, the psalmist cries out to God that his eye takes refuge in the Lord:

Set a guard over my mouth, Lord. Keep watch over the door of my lips. Let not my heart be drawn to the evil thing, to take part in wicked deeds with men doing evil. Let me not eat of their dainties. (Psalm 141:3–5)

But my eyes are fixed on you O Sovereign Lord . . . (Psalm 141:8–9)

The Old Testament tells of Joseph, the beloved son of Jacob, who was indeed the apple of his father's eye.

Jacob loved Joseph more than all his sons . . . and he made for him a richly ornamented robe. When his brothers saw that their father loved him more than all his brothers, they hated him . . . (Genesis 37:3–5)

Jacob gave the coat of many colors to his dearest son, and Joseph thereby became the victim of his brothers' envy. They threw him into a pit and planned to kill him but relented slightly and decided that it would be more profitable to sell him to a passing caravaneer for twenty pieces of silver. Joseph's brothers eyed him with considerable envy. Joseph, because he was able to interpret dreams, eventually became a minister to Pharaoh and a man of considerable power. Many years later, Joseph was able to save his brothers and his father from famine and death. Because Joseph was victorious over the evil eye of his brothers, the passage that Jacob used, just before he died, in blessing Joseph is frequently used as an amulet against the evil eye:

ben porat Yusef . . . Joseph is a fruitful vine, a fruitful vine near a spring, whose branches climb over a wall. (Genesis 49: 22–23)

The word *ayin* means both "eye" and "spring" or "well." The eye-shaped ring pictured in figure 27a is inscribed with the passage from Genesis, *ben porat Yusef*. The eye-shaped rings shown in figure 27 are both protective amulets for warding off the evil eye and benevolent amulets that call forth the benediction of the eye of love.

Because Joseph was loved by his father he was able to trust his inner intuitive eye. The deep unconditional love that Joseph received from his father was indeed like a spring of fresh water, a very valuable resource in a hot and parched land. With all this love inside him he was able to climb over the walls he encountered in his life. When he was a boy, "Joseph had a dream and when he told it to his brothers they increased to hate him more." (Genesis 37:5–6)

The Hebrew word for "increase," *yusfoo*, has the same root as the name Joseph and is an obvious foreshadowing of the blessing he received from his father . . . Joseph as a fruitful vine.

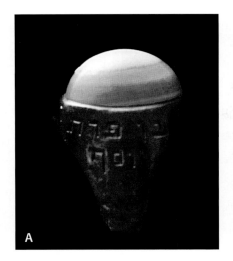

A

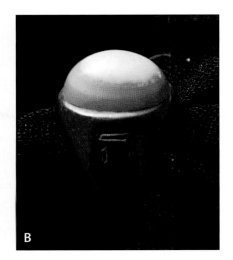

B

C

D

E

Figure 27. Eye rings. The ring in figure 27A has a white moonstone to bind the evil eye, and the protective formula, "Joseph is a fruitful vine." It also has a tiny incised eye on one side of the shank. Figure B shows the other side with the Hebrew letter *heh*, which is the most economical magic name for God. The ring in figure C has a shield with the customary incantation against the evil eye, *Yusef ben porat*. The eye ring in figure D protects against the evil eye with yet another formula. Figure E shows a ring that has a secret formula using letters against the evil eye, and is complete with eyelashes. (Photographs by Junenoire.)

Joseph's dream was that while all the brothers were binding sheaves of grain in the field, Joseph's sheaf suddenly stood upright and his brothers' sheaves bowed down to it. Joseph told this dream to his brothers. And later when he dreamt that the sun and moon and eleven stars also bowed to him, he told this dream to his brothers, and to his father. The Torah comments

> *His brothers were jealous of him but his father kept the matter in his mind.*
> (Genesis 37:11–12)

Clearly Joseph understood his dreams to be objective facts or messages from God. He trusted his understanding of his dreams and valued them. When he was mature, he was able to use this valuable intuitive inner eye to interpret Pharaoh's dreams, and to save the Egyptians and his own people from famine. In many ways, the gifted inner eye is the true amulet against the evil eye of projection.

The eye as a mirror of the soul may be full of love. This eye of love is necessary for the healthy psychological development of a child, while its opposite, the envious evil eye, may damage a baby irrevocably. The Song of Songs verse rings true:

> *Love is as strong as death and jealousy as cruel as the grave . . .*
> (Song of Songs 8:6–7)

One might die from an evil look in the eye of their lover. Eyes wound and eyes seduce and fascinate, and eyes mirror and can heal, as well.

> *The eye never has enough of seeing, or the ear its fill of hearing. What has been will be done again; there is nothing new under the sun.*
> (Ecclesiastes 1:8–10)

Before a betrothal or wedding ceremony in many parts of the world, Jews, as well as Muslims and Hindus—and both men and women—have their palms and soles painted with semi-permanent designs and symbols in henna. These designs are amulets for fertility and protective talismans against evil spirits.

When we are happiest and most fulfilled and complete, the envy of the evil ones is great and we are vulnerable and need protection. When we are taking a step toward the soul's completion, when we are in love, betrothed or

Figure 28. Hands painted with henna.

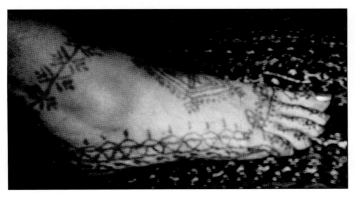

Figure 29. Foot with henna.

Figure 30. Bedouin woman with hennaed hands.

Figure 31. A Yemenite bride in Rehovot, in the 1970s. She wears the traditional regalia of prayer cases, *hamsas*, wedding bracelets, rings, fertility charms, amber and silver beads, henna on hands and fingernails, and kohl around her eyes. (Photo by Barbara Pfeffer. Gift of Barbara Pfeffer, Museum of Jewish Heritage, New York.)

wed, there is much need for protection from the unfinished, incomplete, evil ones. Sometimes the evil ones are truly others, outside one's self, but sometimes the fear and evil feelings are our own unacceptable or unconscious emotions. If our own fear and anger is projected onto others, it is felt as a glance from the evil eye. When fear and anger are seen, understood, and accepted inside into ourselves as our own feelings, we become fruitful, creative vines like Joseph.

Hamsa

The *hamsa*, or five-fingered hand, has a strong protective quality. The image of the hand has been used as a representation of God in all ages and among all people. It was found in Carthaginian excavations and in ancient Egypt where the Great Hand meant the supreme power.

In Muslim countries, the *hamsa* is sometimes called the Hand of Fatima. Fatima is the beloved the daughter of the Prophet Muhammad. She is called *al-Zahara*, "the bright blooming," a name for Venus, and *al-Batul*, "clean maid," or Virgin even after she had become a mother. This is the old meaning of "virgin." It means a woman who is one in herself. The word *hamsa* means five. The five fingers of the one hand held up in loving protection and benediction is used on magical jewelry and on all kinds of amulets by Jews as well as Muslims.

In the Old Testament, the raised hand is an act of worshipping God (Job 31:27). Some of the *hamsas* seen in figure 33 have Kabbalistic signs on them, and many have the magic names for God on them such as *Shaddai*, meaning God Almighty, and *Zamargad,* the realm of demons. The raised hand is part of the hanging lamp that holds the eternal flame in many North African synagogues (see figure 34 on page 56).

Figure 32, facing page. A necklace with many gold *hamsas* and other symbolic amulets against the evil eye. This type of necklace is favored by North African Jewish women.

Figure 33, above. *Hamsas* from the author's collection.

The metal amulet pictured in figure 35 is a virtual supermarket of protection and benevolence. The outer inscription is *shivti*. It means "I will always envision God before me." (Psalm 16:8) The inscription continues along the outer edge with the verse, "Noah was favored by God" (Genesis 6:8–9). The inner second row of text is the incantation against the evil eye, *"ben porat Yusef*—Joseph is a fruitful vine, a fruitful vine near a spring whose branches climb over a wall."* (Genesis 49:22–23)

The third row of text has the word *zamargad* written twice, once on each side of the hand. The word *zamargad* is often used when the word *zamarchad* is intended. Indeed on this particular amulet it may be that one of the words is *zamargad* and the other is *zamarchad*. There is a tiny difference of a bit of a line between the Hebrew letter *gimmel* and the letter *chet*, but there is a world of difference in meaning of the two words.

Figure 34. Moroccan and Tunisian *hamsas* on hanging synagogue lamp holding the eternal flame. (Photograph by Junenoire.)

Figure 35. Amulet with *ben porat Yusef,* the prayer for protection from the evil eye, and a *hamsa* and magic names for God on it.

Zamargad is the realm of the notorious night demon and seductress Lilith, while *zamarchad* is one of the magic names of God. It is made up of the final letters of the first five lines of Genesis 1:1–5. Confusion of the two words is a common mistake made on amulets because of the phonetic resemblance of the two words, and because engravers were often illiterate and may have misheard the instructions of the customer for the amulet. Or, it is also possible that there is really no mistake because there is indeed a mystical connection between the first five lines of creation, and Lilith who was, according to *midrash*, the first woman, and present at the beginning.

THE MYSTIC WAY

It is easy to see why amulets and talismans bearing prayerful words were and are so needed by human beings. Consider, for example, Psalm 121, A Song of Ascents:

I will lift up my eyes to the hills. From where comes my help? My help is from the Lord, Maker of heaven and earth. He will not let your foot slip, he will not slumber, the one guarding you. Behold, he will not slumber and he will not sleep, the one guarding Israel. The Lord is guarding you. The Lord is your shade on your right hand. The sun shall not smite you by day, nor the moon by night. The Lord will guard you from all evil; he will guard your life. The Lord will guard your going out and your coming in from now until forevermore. (Psalm 121)

The song of ascent is an inspiring and hope-filled psalm. When it is coupled with the promise:

If you listen hearken to the voice of the Lord your God, and do that which is right in his eyes, and attend to his commands and keep all his statutes,

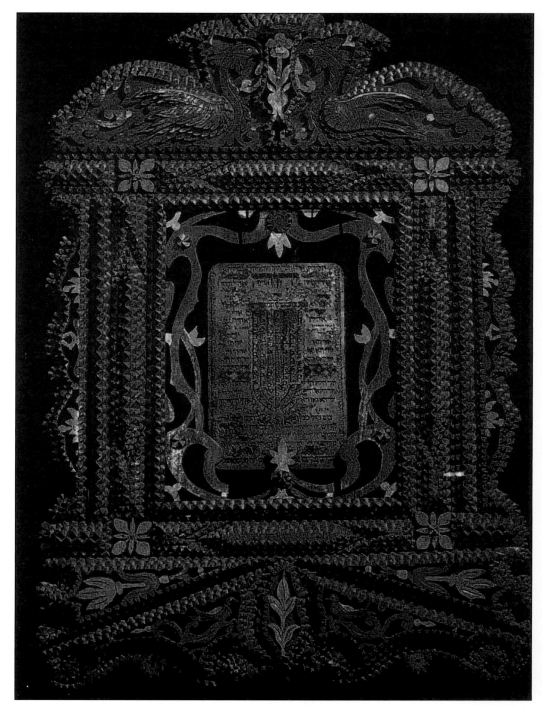

Figure 36. Carved wooden synagogue amulet.

the disease that I brought on the Egyptians, I will not bring on you; for I am the Lord, the one healing you. (Exodus 15:26–27)

The essence of mystical language is that it expands meaning and opens new horizons in imagination, insight, and spiritual quest. Ideas and images from holy scriptures raise our hopes, understanding, insight, and spirit. Magical language, on the other hand, sacrifices meaning in order to affect the heavenly realms. Magical words or sentences will have no accessible meaning, no semantic structure, nor any understandable context on earth, but they are magic formulas that are believed to have meaning in the heavenly realms and for angels. Amulets and talismans carry both mystical prayers and magical formulas.

Letters, Words, and Names

The Hebrew alphabet could easily be called the letters of creation. The word for "letter" is *ot*. It means "a sign," and it also has the connotative meaning of "creation." The process of creation described in the book of Genesis can be interpreted as an endless stream of letters poured from heaven to earth. Thought of in this way, letters bring a thing into being. If there is no written or verbal designation for a thing, it is no thing. Schneur Zalman of Liadi the first Lubuvitcher Rebbe, known as the *alte* Rebbe, writes brilliantly about the letters of creation in *Lessons in Tanya*:

> *God said: Let there be a firmament between the waters . . .* (Genesis 1:6)

> These words and letters through which the heavens were created stand firmly forever within the firmament of heaven. Similarly, every thing created by God must constantly and ceaselessly be vested with

Figure 37. Plastic laminated amulet in use today with the magic names of God and prayers, a *hamsa*, and many protective symbols.

Figure 38. Modern laminated amulet for protection against the evil eye.

the divine life force which created it. If the creative letters were to depart even for an instant and return to their source—God—all the heavens would become naught and absolutely nothingness, and it would be as though they had never existed at all, exactly as before the utterance, *"Let there be a firmament . . ."*[1]

Even within that which appears to be utterly inanimate matter—such as stones or earth or water—there is a soul and spiritual life force. Although they evince no demonstrable form of animation, within them are, nevertheless, the letters of speech from the ten utterances of creation in the Book of Genesis which give life and existence to inanimate matter, enabling it to come into being out of the naught and nothingness that preceded the six days of creation.

The *alte* Rebbe continues:

The name *evan* or stone is not mentioned in the ten utterances. How can we then say that the letters of the ten utterances are enclothed within a stone? He goes on to explain that the twenty-two letters of the Hebrew alphabet in two letter combinations form 462 pairs. Half of these are exact reversals of each other, i.e., *aleph-bet* and *bet-aleph*. The 231 remaining pairs are gates. The names of all creatures in the holy tongue are the very letters of speech which descend degree by degree, from the ten utterances recorded in the Torah. By a process of substitution and transposition the letters pass through the 231 gates until they reach a particular created thing and become invested in it, thereby giving it life.[2]

---

1. Rabbi Schneur Zalman, *Lessons in Tanya*, Vol. III (Brooklyn: Kehot Publication Society, 1991), pp. 838–839.
2. *Lessons in Tanya*, pp. 840–841.

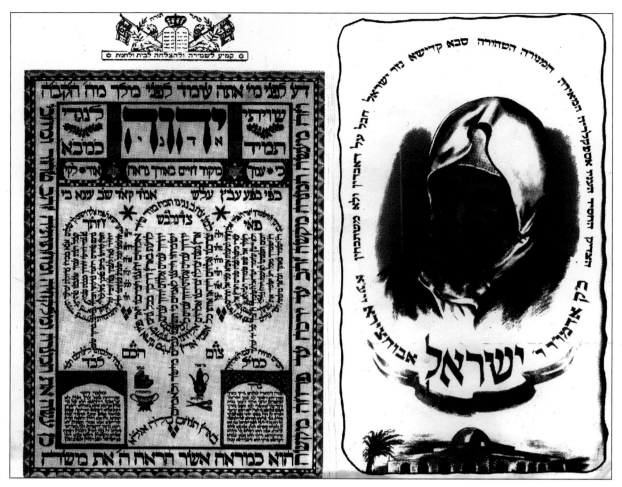

Figure 39. Amulet containing the unutterable name for God, given away on the streets of Jerusalem in the summer of 1999. The beloved Rebbe Baba Salli called the Holy Menorah is pictured.

The amulets shown in the *Sefer Raziel* use the ancient alphabet of the Samaritans, which is the magic alphabet sometimes used in charms even today. While some of the letters are unrecognizable, they resemble Hebrew letters with circles added at the ends and joining of the lines. These are called in Hebrew *ktav malakim*, "angel writing," or *ktav mishkafaiem*, "eyeglass writing." (See figure 40 on page 66.)

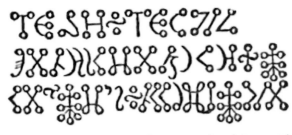

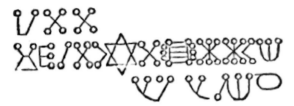

קמיע אחרת לחן ולחסד כתוב על קלף צבי כשר בשמך דחנינא וחסד
יהוה בעולם יהי חסדך יהוה על פב״ם כשם שהיה עם יוסף
הצדיק שנאמר ויהי ה׳ את יוסף ויט עליו חסד ויתן את חנו בעיני כל
רואיו בשם מיכא״ל גבריא״ל רפא״ל אוריא״ל כבשיא״ל יה יה יה יה
יה יה יה אהי״ה   אהה אההה אהה יהו יהו יהו יהו יהו יהו
יהו יהו יה

Figure 40. Angel writing based on ancient Samaritan letters used on an amulet that brings love and friendship to the wearer. According to the *Sefer Raziel*, a book of magic formulas given to Adam, the amulet was written with a copper pen upon a strip of parchment with ink made from lilies and crocuses.

II Kings 17:6 tells that the Samaritans were exiled by Shalmaneser, the king of Assyria, in 722 B.C.E. Between then and the birth of Christ, the Samaritans adopted much of the Jewish religion. They believe that Mount Gerizim near Shechem, rather than the Temple Mount in Jerusalem, was the seat of worship. Like the Hebrews, the Samaritans accepted the one unseen, all-powerful God of the Old Testament. Instead of the words of the usual Hebrew prayer (Hear, O Israel: The Lord our God, the Lord is one . . .) being placed in the *mezuzah* and hung on doorposts and gates, the Samaritans used the ten words of the Ten Commandments. They actually cut the words of the Ten Commandments into the stone gate posts of their houses. Sometimes the ten words of creation, the ten utterances, were used as an amulet or *mezuzah* by the Samaritans. The *totophot*, or phylactery, was worn as an amulet all the time by the Samaritans like a *k'mea* or prayercase, unlike the usual *tefillin,* which traditionally are wound around the arm and forehead only at prayer time. Why the alphabet of the Samaritans is the lettering system used for the amulets shown in the *Sefer Raziel* is a mystery shrouded in the mists of time.

Words of Creation

The palindrome words of Exodus 15:15–16—written in Hebrew from end to beginning with the words, not the letters reversed—are often used on amulets. The last word of verse sixteen and proceeding to the beginning of the first word of verse fifteen shows how the magic of the words and their order can create and destroy:

> *The chiefs of Edom will be terrified, the leaders of Moab will be seized with*
> *trembling, the people of Canaan will melt away; terror and dread will fall*
> *on them. By the power of your arm they will be still as stone until he*
> *crosses over, your people, Lord; until he crosses over, people whom you*
> *bought pass by. (Exodus 15:15–17)*

Another verse showing the power of the word to be an ever present and surrounding experience of the almighty god:

> *Then he withdrew the angel of God, the one traveling in front of the army*
> *of Israel and he went to behind them and he moved, the pillar of cloud from*
> *in front of them, and he stood behind them. (Exodus 14:19–20)*

When God ceased to be a small clay or large stone idol and became an experience of human consciousness the letters or word or name of this experience became vital to its expression.

Names

> *The Lord said to Moses,*
> *Tell Aaron and his sons, This is how you are to bless the Israelites:*

Figure 41. A beautiful Islamic amulet with the name Allah as the central motif.

Say to them,
The Lord bless you and keep you
The Lord make his face to shine upon you,
 and be gracious to you:
The Lord turn his face
 toward you
 and give you peace.
So shall they put my name upon the people of
Israel, and I will bless them.
(Numbers 6:21–27)

The entire Torah, or Law as told in the first five books of Moses in the Hebrew Bible, is called a name of God because it expresses God's creation. The name is what God is. There is one God and many names. Every verse of the Holy Qur'an begins with the words, *Bismillah ir Rachman, ir Rachim,* "In the name of God the Compassionate and the Merciful." Muslims have 99 names for the one God. He is *Jami,* the gatherer, *Nur,* the light, *Haqq,* truth, and *Subhan,* the All Splendiferous.

The tradition of the *Baalei Shem Tov,* or the "masters of the good name," holds that healing and protection come from knowing and using the holy names. The *Hasidim* and *mekubalim* are followers of a mystic path who search for the all-powerful ineffable name of God, the Great Name, or the *Shem Hameforash,* the name which is separate and to be distinguished from every other name for God. King Solomon alone knew this name, and because of this knowledge he was able to construct the great Temple in Jerusalem.

The never-pronounced holy name of God is the *Tetragrammaton yud, heh, vav, heh* or YHWH. This is the name given by God to the children of Israel so that he could take them out of their enslavement in Egypt.

Moses said to God , "Behold, I go to the children of Israel and I say to them, God of your fathers, he sent me to you and they ask to me what is the name of him? What shall I tell to them?" And God said to Moses, "I am who I am" and he said this you shall say to the sons of Israel: "I AM, he sent me to you." (Exodus 3:13–15)

This name is vocalized by adding to it the vowels from the Hebrew word for Lord, *Adonai*. It is also the basis for the words Yahweh and Jehovah. Some Orthodox Jews do not pronounce the name *Adonai* either, but say instead *Ado hem*, or *Ha-Shem*, the name, unless praying, when it is permitted to say the name *Adonai* or the Lord. Even when the Temple in Jerusalem was standing and in active use, the *Tetragrammaton* was pronounced aloud only by the high priest and then only once a year. The single letter *heh* taken from the *Tetragrammaton* is an effective holy name and appears on amulets. The name *Shaddai*—which is also given in the Torah and means "God almighty"—is freely pronounced and used on amulets and *mezuzot*.

The written names of God, the names of the angels, and the words of the Hebrew Bible all have the power to protect human beings from the evil ones. All these names and words are *shemoth*, or Names of God. The power is in the letters and the words. It is derived from the divine source so it is not necessary to write the entire Name or biblical quotation to evoke the protection of the Name.

There are many systems for abbreviating the Names. Sometimes only the first or last letter of each word of a biblical passage is used. Sometimes the first one or two letters of each word in a quotation are used. This form of *serugin*, or trellis, writing carries the protective power of an entire psalm or biblical passage on its trellised structure. Amulets were often made of silver and these magical trellis-written names were frequently used on the relatively small surfaces available on the precious metal amulets.

There are a great many other much more cryptic ways of constructing the Names. Sometimes the first letter of the alphabet is substituted for the last, the second letter for the next to last, and so on. Sometimes the twenty-two-letter Hebrew alphabet is split in half, and the first letter is substituted for

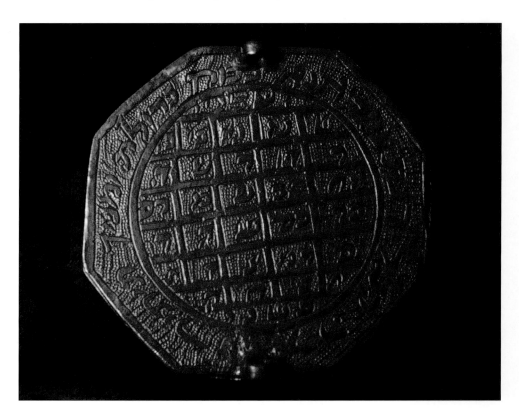

Figure 42. Eight-sided gold amulet with the forty-two letter name of God and twenty-nine boxes containing secret letters on the back. (Photograph by Junenoire.)

the twelfth, the second for the thirteenth and so forth. There are systems of magic boxes containing letters that maybe substituted for one another. Since each letter of the Hebrew alphabet has a numerical value in the process of gematria, one can substitute one word for another entirely different word having the same numerical value. The permutations and possible combinations of words and names of power are dizzying and infinite, and intentionally so in order to convey the sense of the divine dominion over all, and the divine essence in every thing, every letter, and every word.

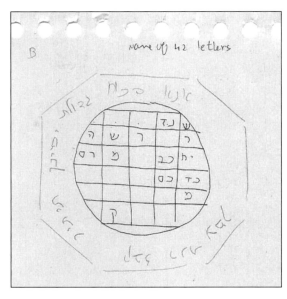

Figure 43. Worksheet for the back of the octagonal amulet with the forty-two letter name with known letters included.

The Kabbalists consider the twelve, the forty-two, and the seventy-two letter names of God to be the *Shem Hameforash*, or the "Ineffable Name of God." The twelve letter Name is made of the first three Sephirot, or attributes of God: *Keter*, or crown, *Chochmah*, or wisdom, and *Binah*, understanding. The seventy-two letter Name begins with *Ain sof*, followed by the forty-two letter Name, and the consonants of the Hebrew word *kodesh* repeated three times, meaning Holy, Holy, Holy, and lastly the Hebrew words meaning "God Most High, maker of heaven and earth." (Genesis 14:19–20) Traditionally, it is said that it was with the seventy-two letter Name that God brought the children of Israel out of Egypt. Psychologically, it means that consciously knowing the many names of the one God will free you from *Mitzriyim*, the narrow place, Egypt.

The letters around the perimeter of the back of the amulet shown in figure 43 are taken from the forty-two word prayer *ana b'koach gedulat*, "We beg you with the strength of your right hand's greatness untie the bundled sins.

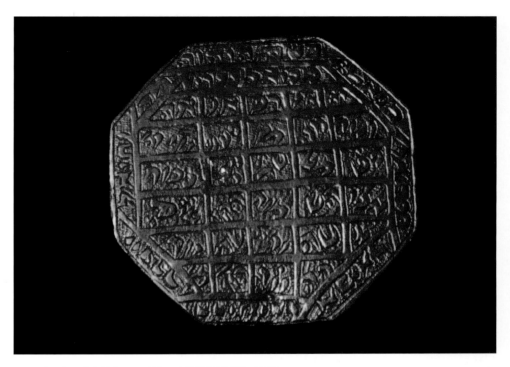

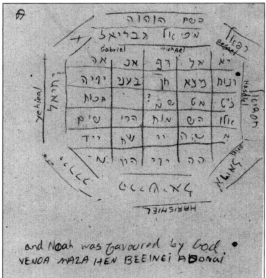

Figure 44. Eight-sided gold amulet with names of angels on front, and squares containing mysterious undeciphered letter formulas. This amulet is used by Persian Jews for protection from evil and illness. The image to the left is a worksheet used to decipher this amulet.

Accept the prayer of your nation; strengthen us, purify us, O awesome one, please O strong one, —those who foster your oneness, guard them like the apple of your eye. Bless them, purify them, show them pity, may your righteousness always recompense them. Powerful holy one, with your abundant goodness guide your congregation. One and only exalted one, turn to your nation which proclaims your holiness. Accept our entreaty and hear our cry, O knower of mysteries."

The initial letters of the forty-two Hebrew words of this mystic prayer are used to form the secret forty-two letter name of God. The six initials of each of the seven verses are also used to form divine names. The Kabbalists teach that the mystic forty-two letter name of God should be divided into phrases of two words each and that this name also contains the names of the ten Sephirot, or divine attributes of God. The outer perimeter of the back of the amulet has the forty-two letter name of God.

Then there are twenty-two boxes, each containing one or two letters. It is not known what these letters mean. They may be the first two letters of a particular verse of Torah or of a psalm, or they may be even more encoded and hidden. The Kabbalists believed that the one letter represents the all. Using only one or two letters increased the focus and intensity of an amulet because it allowed more names for God and the angels to appear on a small amulet.

The front of the same amulet contains the names of the angels Raphael, Michael, Gabriel, Yehieal, Hariseal, Ariel, Hasdiel and one that cannot be read. The *el* or *al* at the end of each of the angel's names means "of God." There are twenty-nine boxes containing letters. The second row of boxed letters contains the words, "and Noah was favored by God," but strangely, none of the other boxed letters seem to be words. So again, the meaning of the letters in the other boxes remains a mystery.

Malachim: Messengers.

At every birth, angels come!

There are myriad angels. The Bible speaks of hosts of angels (Joshua 5:14, 15; I Kings 22:19; Job 25:3) Each blade of grass, and every other animate and inanimate thing on earth as well, is said to have its own angel, and each angel has only one function. Each thing has its angel, its *menueah* or appointed one, or its heavenly deputy. There are evil angels and fallen angels, and angels that are God's deputies. These angels have existed since the beginning and are part of the Eternal Being and the fixed order of the universe. Angels are created anew each time a person performs a *mitzvah*, or one of the 613 commandments. Thus, the emotion or the intention that a person expends in doing a *mitzvah* or holy act creates an angel which is a messenger or a way of reaching out to God. Conversely, angels are also sent from above to the earth below as the angel that wrestled with Jacob, or the three angels that appeared to Abraham, and the one seen by Balaam's ass.

The *Sefer Raziel* gives detailed instructions for the use of particular angels for particular purposes: "Whoever wishes to write an amulet should first write the names of the angels responsible for that particular season." Each angel has a single specific function and power. Mefathiel is the opener of doors. Hasdiel (named on the front of the gold amulet pictured in figure 44), Haniel and Rahmiel are angels of benevolence, grace, and mercy. Zachriel rules memory. Some of the angel names contain a Hebrew root that is related to the angel's function, while other angels' names no longer have a discernible relation to the angels' use on amulets.

The *Zohar*, or *Book of Splendor*, of the Kabbalists lists ten different classes of angels. The most important angels are the *malachim* or archangels Sandalphon and Metatron. Sandalphon is said to have been the visionary

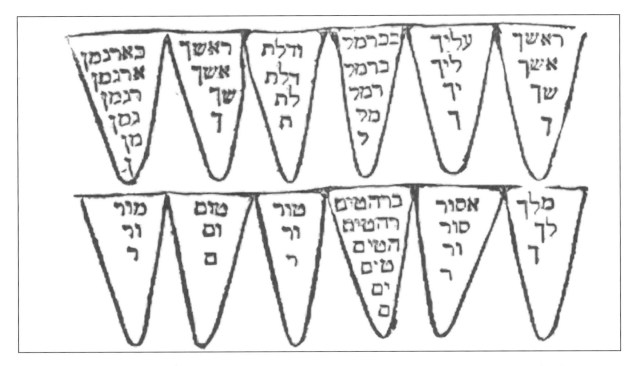

Figure 45. Disappearing word triangle amulet from *Sefer Raziel* using the verse from Song of Songs (7:6-7): "Your head crowns you like the Carmel, and hair of your head like royal purple: a king is held captive in the tresses," containing the magic name *argaman*, a mnemonic for the angels' names Uriel, Raphael, Gabriel, Michael and Nuriel.

Elijah who ascended to heaven in a fiery chariot, and Metatron is thought to be Enoch, who was transported to heaven:

> *Behold, I am sending an angel before you to guard you along the way and to bring you to the place that I prepared. Attend to him and listen to his voice. Rebel not against him for he will not forgive your rebellion for my Name is within him. . . .* (Exodus 23:20–22)

Thus, Metatron is the guardian angel of the children of Israel. The name of the angel Metatron, by the process of gematria, has the same numerical value as the name *Shaddai*, which means "God Almighty." Metatron is in charge of all the other angels and is the master of heavenly song. Metatron will testify to the unity of God on judgment day. The name Metatron along with Sandalphon appears frequently on amulets.

Next in frequency on amulets are the names of the angels: Uriel, Raphael, Gabriel, Michael, and Nuriel. The first four direct the four heavens. The first letter of each name of the angels Uriel, Raphael, Gabriel, Michael, and Nuriel form the Hebrew word *argaman*, which means "purple." The word "purple" appears in the Song of Songs: *Your head crowns you like the Carmel, and the hair of your head like royal purple; a king is held captive in the tresses.* (7:6–7). The mystic meaning of the words "king held captive" in the purple is that God is in the word *argaman*. Thus the word is frequently found on amulets.

The angels of destruction are called the *malache habbala*. Their names end with the letter *peh*. The names of the daily synagogue prayer services, the eighteen benedictions, and the prayer *Yozer Or*—the grace after meals—do not contain this letter. This form of reasoning is a kind of letter magic that is cited as proof that prayer serves as a protection against these destroying angels.

The offspring of fallen angels who have had intercourse with men are called *sheddim*. Among these evil ones are Lilith and her husband Samael. Lilith was Adam's first wife who ran away from him. She returns evermore to seduce men who sleep alone and cause nocturnal emissions. Lilith also strangles newborn babies. The Old Testament offers two accounts of the creation of woman. The demon Lilith was born in the discrepancy between the two. In the first account :

> *God created man in the image of himself, in the image of God he created him, male and female he created them.* (Genesis 1:27–28)

Several verses later:

The Lord God said it is not good for man to be alone. I will make a suitable helpmate for him . . . (Genesis 2:18–19)

So the Lord God made fall a deep sleep upon the man. And he slept. And he took one of the man's ribs and closed up the place with flesh. Then the Lord God made the rib he took from the man into a woman and he brought her to the man. The man said, "This is now bone of my bones and flesh of my flesh. She shall be called woman for she was taken out of man." (Genesis 2:21–24)

The *midrash*, or search for an explanation of what was left out between the two accounts, was offered by the ancient text, the *Alpha Bet ben Sira*:

God formed Lilith, the first woman, just as He had formed Adam, except that He used filth and impure sediment instead of dust or earth. Adam and Lilith never found peace together. She disagreed with him in many matters, and refused to lie beneath him in sexual intercourse, basing her claim for equality on the fact that each had been created from earth. When Lilith saw that Adam would overpower her, she uttered the ineffable name of God and flew up into the air of the world. Eventually, she dwelt in a cave in the desert on the shores of the Red Sea. There she engaged in unbridled promiscuity, consorted with lascivious demons, and gave birth to hundreds of *Lilim,* or demonic babies, daily.

Soon after Lilith left Adam he stood in prayer before his creator and said: "God of the World, woman that you gave me has run away from me." Immediately God, the Holy One, dispatched the three angels Sanvai, Sansanvai, and Smangelof to bring her back. They caught up with her in the desert near the Red Sea. "Return to Adam without delay," the angels said "or we will drown you!"

Figure 46. Amulet from *Sefer Raziel* with names Adam, Eve and the words, "Away from Lilith" above. Below there are two panels containing illustrations of the three angels with their names, Sanvai, Sansanvai, and Smangelof. The panel on the right has the angels' names near their heads, and the panel on the left has the names in the angels' bodies.

"How can I return to Adam after my stay beside the Red Sea?"

"It would be death to refuse," they answered.

"How can I die?" Lilith asked again, "when God has ordered me to take charge of all newborn children: boys up to the eighth day of life, that of circumcision; girls up to the twentieth day." Nevertheless, she said, "I swear to you in the name of God, El, who is living and exists, that if ever I see your three names or likenesses displayed on an amulet above a newborn child, I promise to spare it."

To this they agreed; however, God punished Lilith by making one hundred of her demon children perish daily, and if Lilith could not destroy a human infant, because of the angelic amulet, she would spitefully turn against her own.

The text beneath the drawing on the amulet shown in figure 46 printed upside-down, says that the woman who uses the amulet will be protected by the name *yud, heh, vav, heh* from all the evils and calamities which are enumerated therein. The figures of the angels and their names and seals protected the newborn baby and its mother. The text warded off any and every evil that Lilith might attempt against either one. The five lines of text above the drawings contain the names of the seventy great angels whose protection is secured by this amulet.

ተታብረክ፡ ሎግዚአ፡ እመ
ሑ፡ በዘ፡ መዋ፡ ለክ፡ እዝ
አል፡ መዊ፡ ወናፍ፡ ሰመሑ
ጸ፡ ሐ፡ መዊ፡ ታ፡ ሐጸ፡ መ
ሎ፡ ይተፉ፡ ታ፡ ሕል፡ ሰጐ፡ መ
በ፡ ዝ፡ ዘ፡ ኢ፡ ሀዊም፡ ተ፡ ታ፡ ሐ
በ፡ ዚ፡ ገ፡ ዉ፡ ይ፡ ሠመት፡ ዲ
መ፡ ፀ፡ ተ፡ ሐፍ፡ ለ፡ ብጸ፡
ሮ፡ ክ፡ ዘ፡ ተፉ፡ ገመ፡ ወ፡ ታ፡ ቲ
በ፡ ጠ፡ ሊ፡ ቀብ፡ ዕ፡ ዘ፡ ተ፡ ሐዊ
መ፡ ፋ፡ ታ፡ ሐመ፡ ደ፡ ዩ፡ ወ፡ ነ
ዘ፡ ተ፡ ዉ፡ ግመ፡ ፀ፡ ሕ፡ ሰ፡ ሰ
ገ፡ ሐ፡ ወ፡ ዘ፡ ተ፡ ዱ፡ ግመ፡ ዉ
ሐ፡ መ፡ ዘ፡ ረ፡ ት፡ ዱ፡ ግመ፡ ዉ
ተ፡ ሐ፡ መ፡ ወ፡ ሰ፡ ት፡ ዘ፡ ዊ፡ ገ
ለ፡ ዘ፡ መ፡ ሐ፡ ወ፡ ክ፡ ዘ፡ ዉ፡ ጐ
ወ፡ ተ፡ ሃ፡ ገ፡ መ፡ ወ፡ ተ፡ ሐ፡ ዘ
በ፡ ዘ፡ ግ፡ ወ፡ ዘ፡ ይ፡ ጐ፡ ር፡ ዘ
አ፡ መ፡ ፋ፡ ሐ፡ ወ፡ ዋ፡ ዱ፡ ዩ፡ ጐ
ወ፡ ለ፡ ዉ፡ ዉ፡ ጐ፡ ዘ፡ ወ፡ መ
ዘ፡ ተ፡ ለ፡ መ፡ ዉ፡ ዘ፡ ግ፡ ግ፡ ዉ
ሰ፡ ዋ፡ ገ፡ አግ፡ ጠ፡ ዋ፡ ዘ፡ በ
አ፡ ግ፡ ተ፡ ሐ፡ ፌ፡ ደ፡ ኩ፡ አ፡ ዉ
ዘ፡ በ፡ ወ፡ ዉ፡ ዉ፡ ሐ፡ ክ፡ ዘ
ቲ፡ እ፡ ዬ፡ ዉ፡ ዉ፡ ራ፡ ለ፡ ዱ፡ ለ
ፀ፡ ዉ፡ ዉ፡ ሐ፡ ክ፡ ዉ፡ ወ፡ ዉ
መ፡ ዘ፡ ለ፡ እ፡ ዉ፡ ለ፡ ዘ፡ ዉ፡ ለ
ክ፡ ዘ፡ ዘ፡ ጐ፡ ዱ፡ ዘ፡ ከ፡ ዉ፡ ዉ
ወ፡ ዘ፡ ዉ፡ ዉ፡ ዉ፡ ወ፡ ዘ፡ ዉ
ዘ፡ ዘ፡ ዉ፡ ዉ፡ ዉ፡ ዘ፡ ዉ፡ ዉ
ዘ፡ ዘ፡ ዉ፡ ዘ፡ ዉ፡ ፀ፡ ዘ፡ ዉ
ዘ፡ ዉ፡ ዉ፡ ዉ፡ ዉ፡ ፀ፡ ዉ፡ ዉ

ዉ፡ ት፡ በ፡ ዉ፡ ሐ፡ ዋ፡ ሐ፡ ክ፡ ዉ፡ ክ፡ ዉ፡ ዘ
ፋ፡ ዉ፡ ዘ፡ ዉ፡ ት፡ ዉ፡ ዘ፡ ዉ፡ ዉ፡ ዘ፡ ዉ፡ ዉ
ለ፡ እ፡ ዉ፡ ዘ፡ ዉ፡ መ፡ መ፡ ዉ፡ ዋ፡ ዉ፡ ሰ፡ ዉ
ወ፡ ት፡ ዉ፡ ጠ፡ ዉ፡ ተ፡ ዉ፡ ዉ፡ ዉ፡ ዉ፡ ዉ፡ ጠ፡ ዉ
እ፡ ቶ፡ ዉ፡ ተ፡ ለ፡ ዉ፡ ዉ፡ ዉ፡ ዉ፡ ቀ፡ ዉ፡ ዉ
ለ፡ ዉ፡ ሐ፡ ዉ፡ ዉ፡ ዉ፡ ዉ፡ ዉ፡ ዉ፡ ዉ፡ ዉ፡ ዉ
ራ፡ ት፡ ዉ፡ ተ፡ እ፡ ዉ፡ ዉ፡ ዉ፡ ዉ፡ ዉ፡ ቃ፡ ለ፡ ዉ
እ፡ ዉ፡ ዉ፡ ግ፡ ዉ፡ ጐ፡ ዉ፡ ዉ፡ ዉ፡ ዉ፡ በ፡ ዉ
ለ፡ ዉ፡ መ፡ ዉ፡ ዉ፡ ዘ፡ ዱ፡ ዉ፡ ዉ፡ ለ፡ ዉ፡ ዋ፡ ዉ
ዘ፡ እ፡ ዉ፡ ሐ፡ ዉ፡ ዘ፡ ዉ፡ ዉ፡ ዉ፡ ዉ፡ ዉ፡ ዉ
ጠ፡ ዉ፡ ዱ፡ ፋ፡ ዉ፡ ተ፡ ዉ፡ መ፡ ዉ፡ ዉ፡ ዉ
ለ፡ ዱ፡ ዘ፡ እ፡ ዉ፡ ዉ፡ ወ፡ ዉ፡ ወ፡ ዉ፡ ዉ፡ ዉ
ዉ፡ በ፡ ዉ፡ ዉ፡ ዉ፡ መ፡ ዉ፡ ዉ፡ እ፡ ዉ፡ ት፡ ዉ
ዉ፡ እ፡ ዉ፡ ዉ

WORDS OF POWER 7

The primary function of an amulet or talisman is to ward off the danger that comes from the evil spirits of the middle world. Like prayer, amulets and talismans require focus and intention to be effective. The protective and talismanic function of an amulet depends on certain elements. The letters came first. Then the words. The words are names. The words of Torah, the names of God, the names of the angels, the words of the prayers, and psalms, and often the name of the owner of the amulet are all important. The Bible and other religious rituals identify children as seed of their fathers. When amulets name their owner, the owner is always identified by name, and as the child of its named mother giving value to the old ditty, "Mama's baby, Daddy's, maybe." The last named is the name of a son or daughter of a certain mother who is to benefit from the amulet. Often then—particularly on paper or parchment amulets—*Amen* is written three times and *Selah* three times. The names of God, the names of the particular angels, the exact help that is needed, and the name of the person who needs it are all important on amulets, and sometimes form a dense, almost unreadable whole on the relatively small surface of some precious metal.

Psalms

Carrying the Book of Psalms and reading them upon rising and sleeping is an amulet in itself. There are many instances of soldiers who were shot but lived because the bullet was stopped by a little book of psalms carried in their breast pocket. Psalms, which were originally outpourings of the heart seeking God's help or protection, were often used on amulets. David cries out:

> *Be gracious to me O Lord. For I am withering away; heal me O Lord for my bones are terrified.* (Psalm 6:3–4)

> *I am weary with my sighing; I flood every night my bed: with my tears I moisten my couch.* (Psalm 6:7–8)

Figure 47. A typically tiny book of Psalms. The small size of the book makes it easy to carry around, the hallmark of an amulet.

These Psalms express in words a very personal need for help and protection from an unseen, almighty God. The book *Shimmush Tehillim* describes the magical use of the psalms. It opens with the words: "The entire Torah is composed of the names of God . . ." Meaning that, since the Torah tells of all God's creation, it is *all* the names of God. When the prayers of the heart expressed in the psalms and the names of God as expressed by the word of Torah are combined, they produce a powerful protective amulet.

The Talmud forbids the use of the words of Torah to cure an existing illness but it is permitted to use these words for protection. The underlying principle is that the words themselves have no power to heal, but they may be said in prayer to ask for God's help and protection. A similar distinction is made for the use of amulets. The Jewish sages Maimonides and Ibn Ezra, who were from lands closer to the land of the Bible, were very much opposed to the use of amulets and the reading of Torah verses to cure illness, because these practices bordered on the idolatry of the people of the ancient world who surrounded the children of Israel. Others, including Rashi, who lived in more distant places permitted and encouraged these practices. Regardless of whether their use was encouraged or prohibited, amulets and talismans were used before and during biblical times and are still in use today.

To be sure, a careful distinction is made between amulets and talismans that are valid and permitted, and certain kinds of magic that are forbidden. The underlying principle was, and continues to be, that practices that preceded the Hebrew Bible and were used by the people of Mesopotamia were strongly forbidden because they were based on the idea that each thing was inhabited by its own spirit that needed to be appeased. The effects of this type of sorcery were called *ahizat 'ainayim* or "capturing the eyesight" because they worked by suggestion and idolatry. The acts of the Egyptian magicians described in Exodus 7 are this form of magic, while the acts performed by Moses under God's direction are much more than *ahizat 'ainayim*. They are miracles that capture the heart and mind and go well beyond the eye. The permitted practices are based on the "Laws of Creation" as set forth in the Old Testament. For these practices one needs to call upon God and the angels for help and protection.

Psalm 97 is often written on leather, paper, parchment, or engraved on metal in the form of a seven-branched candlestick and worn on the body. According to the *Zohar*, the seven-branched menorah is a tree of life; the seven branches also represent the seven planets.

Figure 48. This silver *shiviti* amulet is surmounted by the ineffable name of God and contains the passage from Torah that begins *shiviti Adonai negidi tamid— I will envision God in front of me always.* (Psalm 16:8) It has the entire text of Psalm 67, the Torah verse *ben porat Yusef*, for protection from the Evil Eye, and fish for fertility. At the base of the seven-branched candlestick which represents the tree of life is the prayer and Torah portion. *Shma Yisroel, Adonai, Elohenu, Adonai echad . . . Hear O Israel, the Lord our God, The Lord is one.* (Deuteronomy 6:4–6) *. . . Ha -Shem (the Name) will reign, is reigning, and reigned forever and ever. Blessed is the glorious name of his kingdom forever and ever . . .*

The Lord reigns; let the earth be glad; let the many coastlands rejoice!
Clouds and thick darkness surround him; righteousness and justice are the
foundation of his throne. Fire goes before him, and consumes his foes round
about. His lightning lights up the world; the earth sees and trembles. The
mountains melt like wax before the Lord, before the Lord of all the earth.
The heavens proclaim his righteousness; and all the peoples see his glory. All
who worship images are put to shame, those who boast in idols—worship
him all you gods. Zion hears and is glad, and the daughters of Judah rejoice,
because of your judgments, O Lord. For you, O Lord, are most high over all
the earth; you are exalted far above all gods. The ones loving the Lord hate
evil for he guards the lives of his faithful ones; he delivers them from the
hand of the wicked. Light is shed on the
righteous, and joy on the upright in heart.
Rejoice in the Lord, you who are righteous,
and praise his holy name! (Psalm 97:1–12)

The silver *shiviti* amulet pictured in figure 48
contains many elements typical of these
amulets. There is the central placement of the
Tetragrammaton, or ineffable name of God,
and then on the seven branches of the candle-

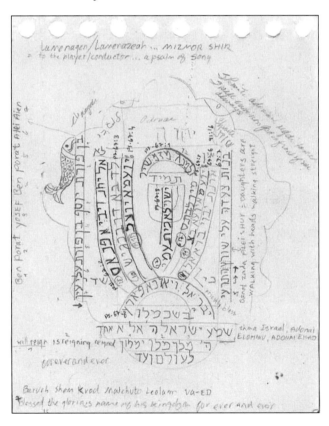

Figure 49. One of the worksheets used to decipher this amulet. The process followed is to draw or trace the shape of the amulet and then to copy as much of the inscription as possible. The inscription is very dense but at a certain point intuition often intervenes or takes over and carries the process of deciphering the amulet to a satisfying conclusion.

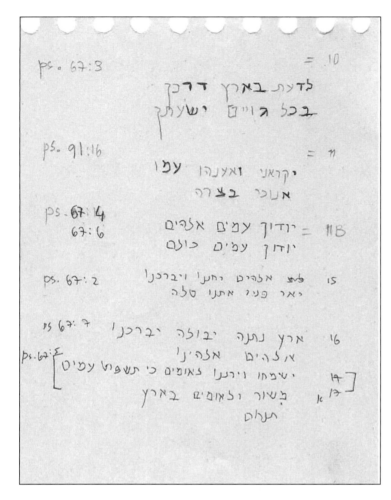

Figure 50. Worksheet 2 for the silver *shiviti* amulet.

stick the complete text of the sixty-seventh psalm:

To the chief musician on Neginoth, a psalm or song.

May God be gracious to us and bless us. May he cause his face to shine upon us, Selah.

That upon earth men may know thy way, among all nations thy salvation.

The people will thank thee, O God; the people, all of them together, will thank thee!

Nations will be glad and sing for joy, when you judge the people righteously, and guide the nations upon earth. Selah.

The people will thank thee, O God; the people, all of them together, will thank thee.

The earth has yielded her products: yes. God, our God, will bless us. God will bless us; and all the ends of the earth shall fear him
(Psalm 67:1–7)

BE FRUITFUL AND MULTIPLY

ne of the promises made by the unseen ever-present God to his followers was to increase fertility and to prevent miscarriage:

You will be blessed more than any other people, none of your men or women will be childless . . . (Deuteronomy 7:14)

. . . and none will miscarry or be barren in your land . . . (Exodus 23:26)

Not surprisingly, fertility was a great concern for the survival of the people of the ancient world. Even today, help in these matters continues to be needed. The silver *shiviti* amulet shown in figure 48 was purchased by a woman who believed it was for help in becoming pregnant. She had been trying to conceive for seventeen lunar months. During the first cycle in which she wore the amulet, her prayers were answered.

After the invocation of the names of God and the angels, an amulet usually a contains a biblical verse chosen for a specific purpose. Beyond the general protection of the names of God, amulets are often needed to bring love

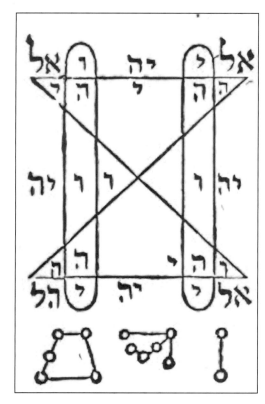

Figure 51. Love amulet from *Sefer Raziel*.

and fertility. The amulet shown in figure 51 contains only the two names *el* and *yud, heh, vav, heh*, but nevertheless it is a powerful amulet shown in the *Sefer Raziel* and guaranteed to bring love to the wearer.

According to the *Sefer Raziel*, this amulet is for love between the man and his wife or between a man and his friend. It also relates to loving God with all your heart and with all your soul (Deuteronomy 6:5–6).

The *Sefer Raziel* continues translating the love amulet: "It should be your will *Heh*, this is the name for God that means *chesed* or loving kindness, and God of our fathers, to send your holy angels face to face for the purpose of love between them. These are the names of the angels who are charged with love: *Pitshata, Matzpatz, Tachtzmal* . . . They shall put love and brotherliness in the way of confrontation and there will not be hate or jealousy or animated dispute and no bad thing—-except a whole heart and love and brotherliness from today and forever. It is necessary for this to be the depiction." "This" refers to the diagram pictured above.

Meditation on this diagram will bring a person love and help him or her avoid conflict with others. How can this happen? The amulet contains only a few lines and words—two names for God—*El* and *yud, heh, vav, heh*, the ineffable name. Nevertheless, the *Sefer Raziel* says it means all that is written above. The two parallel figures and the intersecting lines and formal balance of the diagram are striking. The interpretation from the *Sefer Raziel* uses an abbreviation for the words "face to face" twice. The image of "face to face" is used for the relationship of love and for the relationship of confrontation. In

Hebrew, the same word means both "mouth" and "face." The diagram does become more meaningful as one studies it and gives eyes and mind and heart to understanding it.

Each angel can do only one thing. Angels are focused energy and messengers. They carry a human being's message of prayer or intention and need to the heavens above and they are also messengers of God's intention and protection. The story of the meeting between the prophet Elijah and the seductress and child-killing demon Lilith illustrates the continuous interaction between the upper world and the lower, and the powers of good and evil:

Once upon a time the prophet Elijah was walking along the road when he encountered the wicked Lilith accompanied by all her gang.

"Whither away, foul creature," he demanded, "thou and all thy foul gang?"

"Sire," she replied "I am off to the house of Mistress X who is expecting a child. I am going to plunge her into the sleep of death, take away her babe, suck its blood, drain its marrow and seal up its flesh."

"Nay," cried the prophet. "By the curse of God thou shalt be restrained and turned to dumb stone!"

"Not that!" implored the hag. "For God's sake, release me from that curse, and I will flee; and I will swear unto thee in the name of Jehovah, God of the armies of Israel, to forgo my intent against yon woman and her child. Moreover, when ever in future men recite my names, or I see them written up, neither I nor my gang shall have power to harm or hurt. And these are my names:

"Lilith, Abitr, Abito, Amorfo, Khods. Ikpodo, Ayylo, Prota, Abnukta, Strine, Kle, Ptuza, Tltoi, Pritsa."

Figure 52. Silver amulet with three angels for protection against the seductress and child-killer Lilith. Paradoxically, this Lilith amulet also serves to increase fertility.

It is not surprising that an amulet bearing the names of the angels God sent to bring Lilith back to Adam, and the many names of Lilith, would be effective as an amulet that would bring both fertility and easy, happy births. The amulet shown in figure 46 on page 78 has two compartments showing the three angels Sanvai, Sansanvai, and Smangelof twice, and has the many names of Lilith listed, as well.

Figure 53. Paper amulet for protection against Lilith. The striped figures at the bottom bear the names of the three angels Sanvai, Sansanvai, and Smangelof.

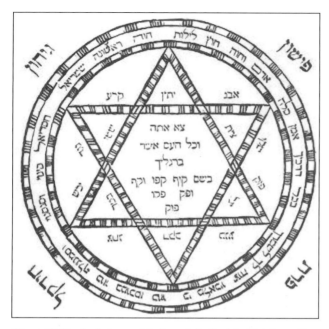

Figure 54. Magic circle amulets from *Sefer Raziel* with intersecting triangles to protect against Lilith.

Women who are not able to afford metal or silver amulets frequently have magic circle amulets chalked on the walls or the floor of the room in which they give birth. Often the newborn baby is also protected from Lilith with a circlet of red thread tied around its wrist as soon as it is born. Sometimes a red string is tied onto or all around the newborn's cradle. Between the two circles seen in the amulet in figure 54 are the names Adam, Eve, Lilith (sometimes called the first Eve), the names of the angels Khasdiel, Sanvai, Sansanvai, Smangelof, and the words "He hath given his angels charge concerning thee, that they may keep thee in all thy ways. Amen, Selah." Outside the circle are the names of the four rivers of paradise: Pishon, Gihon, Prath, and Hiddekel.

Lilith is not only a danger to women in childbirth and to newborn babies, but she was called the night hag who brought disease, nightmares, and death in the night. Psalm 121 says:

The sun shall not smite thee by day, nor the moon by night . . .
(Psalm 121:6–7)

This verse was frequently used on amulets for protection against Lilith as the seductive and death-dealing evil spirit of the night. Similarly, Psalm 91 and, most especially, verse 5–7 were used on amulets to protect against the night demon Lilith:

He who dwells in the shelter of the Most High, will rest in the shadow of
the Almighty. I will say of the Lord, "He is my refuge and my fortress; my
God, in whom I trust. Surely he will save you from the snare of the fowler
and from the deadly pestilence; he will cover you with his feathers, and
under his wings you will find refuge; his faithfulness will be your shield
and rampart.

You will not fear the terror of the night, nor the arrow that flies by day, nor
the pestilence that stalks in darkness, nor
the plague that strikes at noonday.

Thou shalt not be afraid for the terror
by night;

A thousand may fall at your side, ten thousand at your right hand; but it will not
come near you. You will only look with
your eyes and see the punishment of the
wicked. If you make the most high your
dwelling even the Lord, who is my refuge
no harm will befall you, no disaster will
come near your tent. For he will command
his angels concerning you to guard you in
all your ways. (Psalm 91:1–12)

Figure 55. Amulet against nightmares. The magic square contains the
initial letter of each of the first four words of Psalm 91:5—

Thou shalt not be afraid for the terror by night;

לֹא־תִירָא מִפַּחַד לָיְלָה מֵחֵץ

The letters are arranged from right to left as Hebrew is written, and
then they continue and reverse, snaking throughout the amulet, magically making Lilith, serpent and demoness of the night, disappear.

PART THREE

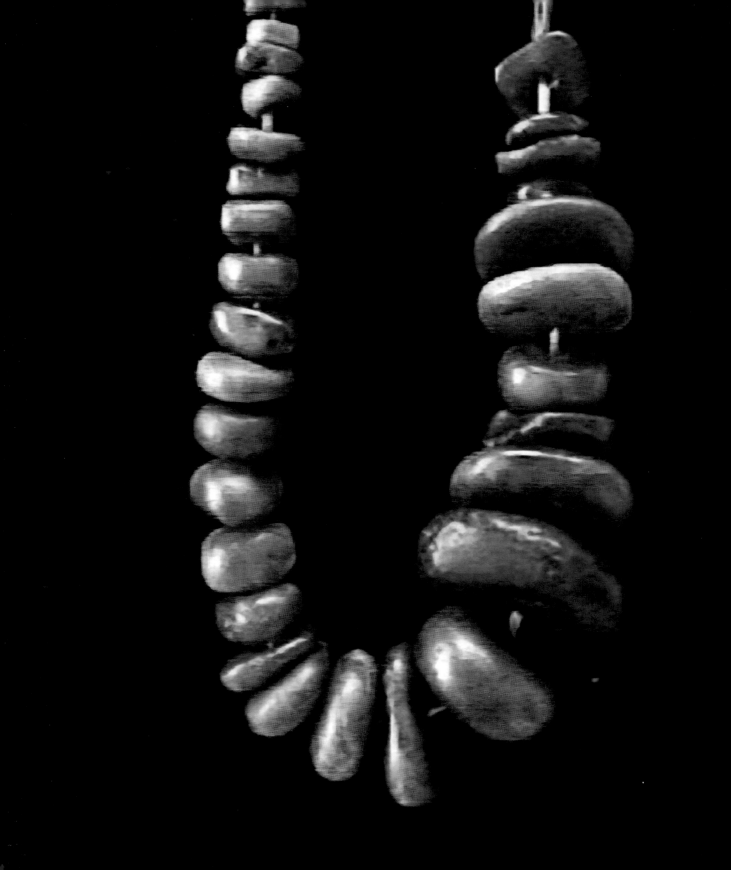

MAGICAL OBJECTS

9

The Gemara in Bava Basra, a commentary on the Old Testament story of Abraham, says that Abraham had a precious stone which he wore around his neck. All those who were ill and looked at this necklace were cured. Abraham was renowned for his loving kindness and hospitality. As he sat in the doorway of his tent while recovering from his circumcision, he saw three men approaching and ran out to greet them. His generous hospitality was given long before they identified themselves as angels of God. According to the Hassidic Rabbis these two *mitzvot* or commandments are ones that we must do with everything we have, all of our possessions. The words *chesed*, "kindness" (*chet, samekh, dalet*) and the word *orayach*, "guest" (*aleph, vav, resh, chet*) when added together equal the gematria of the word *rofeh*, or "healer" (*resh, vav, pey, alef*). When God blessed Abraham, he blessed him with the power of healing, which is one of the three things that are a perfect blessing. Thus the magic object, the healing stone that Abraham is said to have worn around his neck, derives its healing power from his behavior. By obeying God's commandments to be kind and hospitable to strangers he transmits healing love.

In that day the Lord will take away their finery: the bangles and head-bands and crescent necklaces, the earrings and bracelets and veils, the head-dresses and ankle chains and sashes, the perfume bottles and charms (l'hashim) the signet rings and nose rings, the fine robes and the capes and cloaks, the purses and mirrors and the linen garments and tiaras and shawls. (Isaiah 3:20)

The prophet Isaiah warns that, on the day of judgment, all *l'hashim*—the objects or ornaments used in conjunction with whispering incantations, spells, charms, and prayers—will be taken from the people by God. These are objects that are used as the Egyptian magicians used their magic objects—to fool and trick the eye. They are objects of power, not objects used with a full and conscious understanding that the real source of power is the unseen, ever-present God. The Old Testament is rife with examples of magic and miracles. There is, in the book of Exodus, the contest between Moses and the Egyptian magicians:

And the Lord said to Moses, "See, I make you as God to Pharaoh; and Aaron your brother shall be your prophet. You shall speak all that I command you; and Aaron your brother shall tell Pharaoh to let the people of Israel go out of his land. But I will harden Pharaoh's heart, and though I multiply my signs and wonders in the land of Egypt, Pharaoh will not listen to you; then I will lay my hand upon Egypt and bring forth my hosts, my people the sons of Israel, out of the land of Egypt by great acts of judgment. And the Egyptians shall know that I am the Lord, when I stretch forth my hand upon Egypt and bring out the people of Israel from among them."

And Moses and Aaron did so; they did as the Lord commanded them. Now Moses was eighty years old, and Aaron eighty- three years old, when they spoke to Pharaoh. And the Lord said to Moses and Aaron,

"When Pharaoh says to you, 'Prove yourselves by working a miracle,' then you shall say to Aaron, 'Take your rod and cast it down before Pharaoh, that it may become a serpent.' So Moses and Aaron went to Pharaoh and did as the Lord commanded; Aaron cast down his rod before Pharaoh and his servants, and it became a serpent. Then Pharaoh summoned the wise men and the sorcerers; and they also, the magicians of Egypt, did the same by their secret arts. For every man cast down his rod, and they became ser- pents. But Aaron's rod swallowed up their rods. Still Pharaoh's heart was hardened, and he would not listen to them; as the Lord had said.

Then the Lord said to Moses, "Pharaoh's heart is hardened, he refuses to let the people go. Go to Pharaoh in the morning, as he is going out to the water; wait for him by the river's brink, and take in your hand the rod which was turned into a serpent. And you shall say to him, The Lord, the God of the Hebrews, sent me to you, saying, 'Let my people go, that they may serve me in the wilderness; and behold, you have not yet obeyed.' Thus says the Lord, 'By this you shall know that I am the Lord: behold, I will strike the water that is in the Nile with the rod that is in my hand, and it shall be turned to blood, and the fish in the Nile shall die, and the Nile shall become foul, and the Egyptians will loathe to drink water from the Nile.'"

And the Lord said to Moses, "Say to Aaron, 'Take your rod and stretch out your hand over the waters of Egypt, over their rivers, their canals, and their ponds, and all their pools of water, that they may become blood; and there shall be blood throughout all the land of Egypt, both in vessels of wood and in vessels of stone.'"

Moses and Aaron did as the Lord commanded; in the sight of Pharaoh and in the sight of his servants, he lifted up the rod and struck the water that was in the Nile, and all the water that was in the Nile turned to blood. And the fish in the Nile died; and the Nile became foul, so that the Egyptians could not drink water from the Nile; and there was blood throughout all the land of Egypt.

But the magicians of Egypt did the same by their secret arts; so Pharaoh's heart remained hardened, and he would not listen to them; as the Lord had said. Pharaoh turned and went into his house, and he did not lay even this to heart. And all the Egyptians dug round about the Nile for water to drink, for they could not drink the water of the Nile. Seven days passed after the Lord had struck the Nile.
(Exodus 7:1–25)

The contest continues for a while. The Lord tells Aaron to bring frogs, and the Egyptian magicians do the same. Then the Lord tells Aaron to bring gnats, but the Egyptian magicians are unable to make them disappear. The plagues continue, and eventually the unseen, ever-present God is able to bring the children of Israel out of the land of Egypt, or *Mitzriyim*, the narrow place. In Egypt all power rested with Pharaoh. He was a God, a king, and a man. Everyone had to obey him in all matters.

Several passages earlier, the story of Moses' encounter with God and the burning bush is told:

Now Moses was keeping the flock of his father-in-law, Jethro, the priest of Midian; and he led his flock to the west side of the wilderness, and came to Horeb, the mountain of God.

And the angel of the Lord appeared to him in a flame of fire out of the midst of a bush; and he looked, and lo, the bush was burning, yet it was not consumed.

And Moses said, "I will turn aside and see this great sight, why the bush is not burnt."

When the Lord saw that he turned aside to see, God called to him out of the bush, "Moses, Moses!" And he said, "Here am I."

Then he said, "Do not come near; put off your shoes from your feet, for the place on which you are standing is holy ground."

And he said, "I am the God of your father, the God of Abraham, the God of Isaac, and the God of Jacob." And Moses hid his face, for he was afraid to look at God. (Exodus 3: 1–7)

Here is an amazing contrast between the old narrow way of Egypt where there is no free will at all and the new way where there is a wide and free inter-active relationship with the unseen, ever-present God. The word for *see* is used in all its many ways in this passage. It is a full description of the new consciousness that is called for in monotheism.

When the Bible says, "The angel of the Lord appeared," the word for "appeared" is in a form that means that the Lord Himself appeared to Moses.

Moses " had looked" at this mystery, something that burns but is not consumed, but when he "turned aside" he showed a personal intention to really see and understand that goes far beyond mere looking. When the unseen God sees that Moses wants to see, God becomes manifest and says "Here am I."

When Moses is instructed to remove his sandals, we are reminded that when we turn aside from the habitual path, and take an intentional step in a new direction off the well-trodden path, and when we remove ourselves from a habitual standpoint and a habitual way of seeing, we are indeed standing upon holy ground.

The words, "I am the God of your father, the God of Abraham, the God of Isaac, and the God of Jacob" mean that this new form of God is different for each person. He appears differently to Moses' father and to Abraham, and Isaac, and Jacob because each man is required to have a different personal and individual experience of this new unseen, ever-present God. "And Moses hid his face, for he was afraid to look at God . . ." because he was still too afraid of the personal responsibility that the new way entailed.

Amulets and talismans are used to bridge the sense of separation and fear that accompanies the way of individuation. The simple magic square amulet contains letters whose number values by the process of gematria add up to fifteen when added in rows or columns or diagonally. At the heart of the magic square is the letter *heh* an abbreviation for the ineffable name of God (see figure 56).

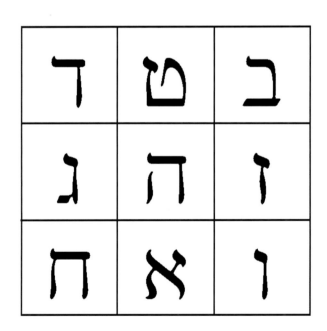

Figure 56. Magic square with *heh* (5) at the heart.

This form of number and letter magic has an internal logic that is intuitively satisfying and reassuring. There are endless variations and permutations of these amulets, but all center on the miraculous, the unseen, understood mystery, and not on mere magic.

Symbolism and Sympathetic Magic

A sign points toward something or names it, and may even bring it forth from being no thing in its unnamed obscurity. When a thing undergoes certain processes of transformation, apprehension, and understanding, it becomes a symbol. The symbol is our best approximation of the thing with all its many meanings. Sympathetic magic relies upon both signs and symbols. In the book of Genesis, Jacob sees Rachel, kisses her, and falls immediately in love with her. Laban, her father, makes Jacob work for seven years as a bride price for Rachel, and then substitutes Rachel's sister Leah—who was not beautiful, and who was older—as the bride of Jacob. Laban demands another seven years of service from Jacob before he finally gives Rachel to her beloved Jacob as a bride. Leah conceives easily and bears Jacob many sons. Rachel does not conceive and in desperation begs Leah to give her the mandrake root found by Leah's oldest son, Reuben. With this powerful fertility charm Rachel is able to conceive and gives birth to Joseph who later becomes the great interpreter of dreams. (Genesis 30:14–22)

Figure 57. Mandrake root. This etching from *Florilegium Renovatum et Auctum* by Johannes Theodorus de Bry, eldest son of the famous German engraver, and published at Frankfurt-on-Main in 1641.

Figure 58. A plastic bag containing seven types of first fruits that come from the area near the tomb at Meron of Rabbi Simeon bar Yohai, author of the *Zohar or Book of Splendor*

Soon afterward, as Jacob prepares to leave Laban's place and return to his own homeland with his wives and children and flocks, Laban again delays him, and says that Jacob may only leave with the striped and speckled goats of the flock. Jacob peels the bark off several branches in strips making a striped pattern on the sticks. Then he puts the striped sticks over the watering place of the animals. The striped and speckled goats reproduce far more plentifully than the solid colored ones. (Genesis 30:37–39)

Both of these incidents are powerful examples of sympathetic magic. Because the mandrake root looks like a male sexual organ it is thought to be a potent fertility charm and possession of it allows Rachel to conceive. Similarly, the striped branches caused the increased fertility of the striped goats. This sort of simple visual magic—where like brings like—can be very effective in certain situations.

The plastic bag pictured in figure 58 contains seven types of first fruits from an area near the tomb of Rabbi Simeon bar Yohai, the author of the *Zohar*. The seven species of first fruits were brought to the temple in Jerusalem as a thanks offering. The writing on the amulet says that it is a healing cure for the evil eye, for health, for prosperity, loss of memory, and for peace in the house. Again like brings like. The wisdom and healing of the great Rebbe is contained in the seven species because they come from the area near the tomb of the great rabbi.

The label on the bottle seen in figure 59 says that it contains special, pure, healing olive oil from olive trees near the tomb of the divine *Tanah*, Rabbi Simeon bar Yohai. The word *Tanah* means "sage" or "teacher." It is from the Hebrew word *Mishnah,* which means to "study and re-study." Rabbi Simeon bar Yohai was a *Tanah* because he studied and taught in A.D. 200 or in the period of the *Mishnah.* The amulet says, "By this prescription you will receive prosperity, success, and anything your heart wishes. This is due to the right of the holy *Tanah.*" Because the teachings of the *Tanah* were healing, the oil from the trees near his tomb are healing.

Reducing letter amulets like the one shown in figure 45 on page 75, where the evil spirits are sent away as the letters and words diminish, and the famous abracadabra formula shown on page 106 in figure 61 are also based on the principle of sympathetic magic.

Figure 59. Healing olive oil from olive tree near the tomb of Rabbi Simeon bar Yohai at Meron.

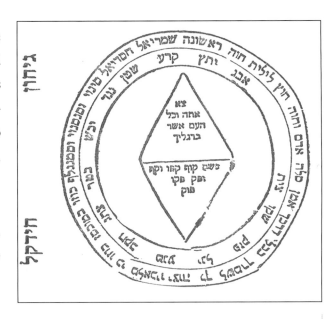

Figure 60. Amulet from the *Sefer Raziel* containing two triangles base to base and the words *go forth thou and all the people who are in thy train.*

```
          A
        R   A
      B   R   A
    A   B   R   A
  D   A   B   R   A
A   D   A   B   R   A
  C   A   D   A   B   R   A
A   C   A   D   A   B   R   A
  R   A   C   A   D   A   B   R   A
B   R   A   C   A   D   A   B   R   A
A B R A C A D A B R A
B   R   A   C   A   D   A   B   R   A
  R   A   C   A   D   A   B   R   A
A   C   A   D   A   B   R   A
  C   A   D   A   B   R   A
    A   D   A   B   R   A
      D   A   B   R   A
        A   B   R   A
          B   R   A
            R   A
              A
```

Figure 61. Disappearing word amulet—two triangles containing the formula: Abracadabra.

FLEE LIKE THESE WORDS . . . .

The Chaldee words *Abbada Ke Dabbra* were addressed to a fever, and mean "Perish like the word." The device of using triangles with the entire word at the top and one letter less in each line is a well known magic device. Two triangles double the potency of the amulet. The command to the evil spirit, "Flee like these words" grows stronger with the upper triangle, and the power of the evil spirit is reduced by the reduction of the letters in the lower triangle. It is believed that by gradually reducing the size of the individual words in an incantation, the evil spirit is eased out of its victim, and its influence is reduced as the words themselves become diminished.

The triangle alone without letters or words is frequently used as a protective amulet. The small beaded triangles seen in figure 62 were pinned on babies in the Muslim parts of Yugoslavia as recently as thirty years ago. Babies are particularly in need of protection from the evil spirits because the evil ones are jealous of the happiness of human beings and they tend to strike when humans are at crossroads, ill, young, or for any reason in a weakened state. These small triangular amulets were pinned on my two-year-old daughter by a total stranger who thought we were neglectful parents because our daughter had no amulets to protect her. Triangles are also protection against the evil eye. The visual resemblance to eyes of the triangle shape and the bead work itself use the principle of sympathetic magic, or homeopathy, to empower the amulet.

The intersecting triangles of the *magen* David, or "shield" of David, are based on the same principle of triangles reducing the power of evil spirits and focusing the protective power of the amulet. The number three and its square, nine are also believed to be powerful magic numbers. The protective shield is formed by the focused energy of the downward pointing triangle and the strength of the upward facing triangle standing on its base. The two triangles also represent the heavenly upper word and the earthly lower world.

The *Sefer Raziel* says that the amulet seen in figure 63 can be used to profit from a negotiation with another person. It says that you must write the diagram and words on a card, and then you must hang it on your left side. You must ride on truthful things: humbleness, your Torah teachings, and the terrible law on your right side. The diagram contains the letters *lamed, tzaddi, chet* in three combinations, and the letter *aleph* for *Amen* twice. There is also the ineffable name of God. The *magen* David have the name *Shaddai*, or "Almighty" at the center, and the ineffable name *yud, heh, vav, heh* in each of the four corner triangles of the shield.

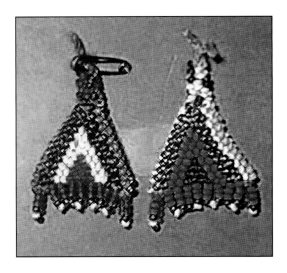

Figure 62. A woman pinned these small protective triangle amulets onto the clothes of the author's two-year-old daughter in Sarajevo in 1969.

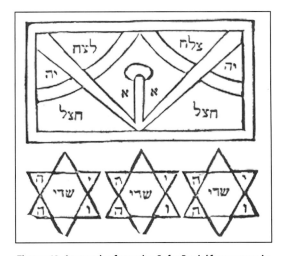

Figure 63. An amulet from the *Sefer Raziel* for success in business containing magic names for God and the *magen* David, with the magic name *Shaddai*, almighty God.

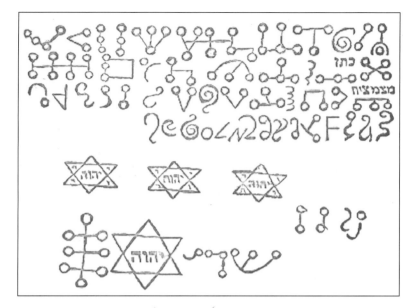

Figure 64. Amulet from *Sefer Raziel* with a *magen* David, and magic names of God to protect the wearer from enemies and injury from lethal weapons.

The two equilateral triangles, one inverted and overlapping the other, may have been adopted by King David as the symbol of his royal house. It was used by the Hebrew tribes long before the time of David. According to legend Moses used a six-pointed star as a prayer amulet—*vat ish ka* or, "she died out"—to put out the fire of God's anger at a place he later called Taberah:

> Now the people complained about their hardships in the hearing of the
> Lord, and when he heard them his anger was aroused. Then fire from the
> Lord burned among them and consumed some of the outskirts of the camp.
> When the people cried out to Moses, he prayed to the Lord and the fire died
> down . . . (Numbers 11:1–3)

Moses made an amulet by drawing a six-pointed star on one side of a piece of parchment with four letters written at the center. They were the initial letters *aleph, gimmel, lamed, aleph* of the four words which mean, "You are mighty forever Adonai." On the reverse side of the amulet was written the diminishing word formula, *vat ish ka* . . . "and the fire died down."

Sympathetic magic plays a part in the use of pictorial elements such as hands, eyes, serpents, circles, locks, knives, birds, animals, fish, and fruit as amulets.

Figure 65. A collection of *magen* David, or shields of David.

Figure 66. Knife amulet for protection from Lilith, and to "cut" the pain of childbirth.

Figure 67. Heart-shaped lock as love amulets Love unlocks the heart.

Figure 68. A beautiful woman's face incised on a heart-shaped lock love amulet from Persia.

As I mentioned earlier, women in the throes of childbirth often placed a knife on their pillow to cut the labor pains and to protect against the demonic, child-killing Lilith. The knife amulet seen above also carries the verse: "I look for your deliverance O Lord." (Genesis 49:18)

The word *argaman* also appears. It is the mnemonic for the angels' names Uriel, Raphael, Gabriel, Michael, and Nuriel, and assures their protection for the bearer of the amulet. The handle of the knife bears the names of Sanvai and Sansanvai and the guard has the name Smangelof. These are the three angels sent by God to bring Lilith back to Adam.

Figure 69. Amulet with a heart enclosed in a triangle and the words *Ma'sAllah*, meaning, if God wills it. This sort of amulet is used in Turkey for the protection and support for a football team. The birds, like angels, carry the message aloft!

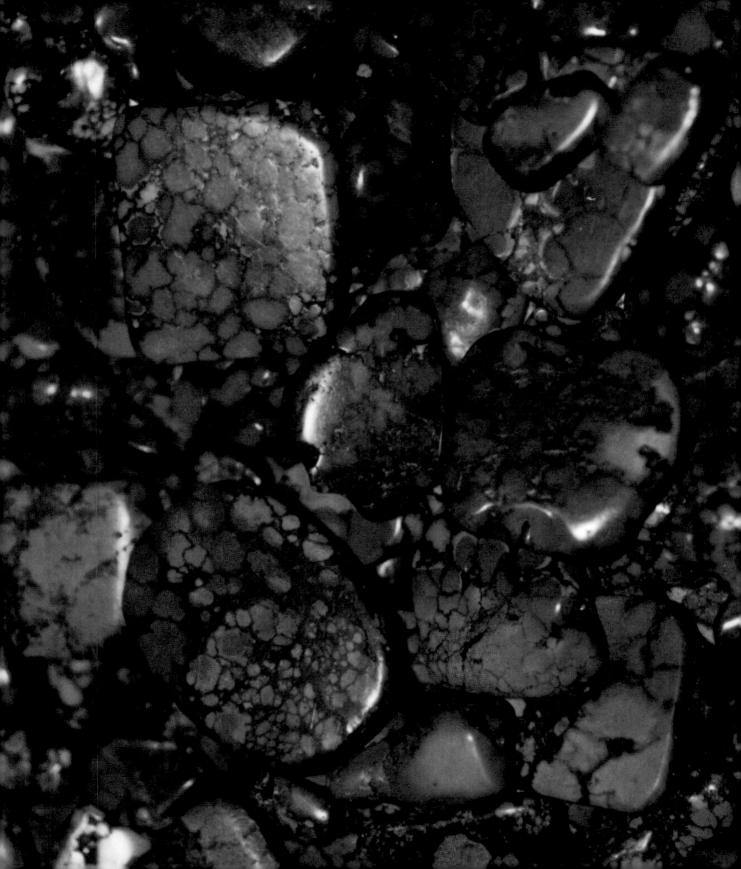

THE SPIRIT IN GEMSTONES

Three thousand years before the establishment of the unseen, ever-present God of monotheism in the lands between the Mediterranean Sea and the Persian Gulf, religious beliefs and esoteric knowledge about amulets were accumulated by the Assyrians, Persians, Arabs, Phoenicians, and Gnostics. The Old Testament abounds with references to the borrowed and continued use of these amulets by the Children of Israel. The *mezuzah*, the *totophot*, the *tzitzis*, and the magical jewelry of the high priest are all prescribed by the Hebrew Bible, and all also show strong connections to these earlier cultures. The *ephod* and the breast piece, the bells at the hem of the robe of the high priest, and the plate of pure gold that is bound to the high priest's turban all have roots in earlier times when these objects were thought to actually contain the spirit of the gods.

The breast piece of the high priest is made of three rows of four gemstones described in the book of Exodus (28:17–22). The Jewish historian Josephus, who lived in the first century (A.D. 37–95) must have seen the high priest wearing the *ephod* and the breast piece, and he described the exceptional size and miraculous powers of the stones:

From the stones which the high priest wore (these were sardonyxes, and I hold it superfluous to describe their nature, since it is known to all), there emanated a light, as often as God was present at the sacrifices; that which was worn on the right shoulder instead of a clasp emitting a radiance sufficient to give light even to those far away, although the stone previously lacked this splendor. And certainly this in itself merits the wonder of all those who do not, out of contempt for religion, allow themselves to be led away by a pretense of wisdom. However, I am about to relate something still more wonderful, namely, that God announced victory in battle by means of the twelve stones worn by the priest on his breast, set in the pectoral. For such a splendor shone from them when the army was not yet in motion, that all the people knew that God himself was present to aid them.[3]

Many legends have grown up over the years about these gemstones. It is said that Moses used the miraculous *shamir* to engrave the names of the twelve tribes of Israel on the hard stones. The names were first written on the gems in ink and then the *shamir* was passed over them. The writing was thus engraved on the stones, and magically, no particles of the gemstones were removed or lost. This very same *shamir* was later used by Solomon to cut the huge stones used to build the holy temple in Jerusalem.

There have been many attempts to trace the modern names and colors for the gems of the breast piece named in Hebrew in the Bible. The treatise on precious stones by Theophrastus (300 B.C.), *The Natural History of Pliny*, the Greek Septuagint and the Latin Vulgate, Josephus and the Rabbinical com-

---

3. Josephus Flavius, *The Antiquities of the Jews*, William Whiston, trans. (London: George Routledge & Sons, Ltd., ca. 1900).

mentary in the *Midrash Bamidbar* on Numbers, are all sources for this speculation. Interest centers on the color of each of the gemstones because by the principle of sympathetic magic, the breast piece's particular power is derived from the color of the stone. Thus *odem*, which is derived from the word meaning "red" was probably a red stone, a carnelian or red jasper, and beneficial for the blood. The *pitdah* seems to be derived from the Sanskrit word for yellow and may be a topaz or light green peridot. The third stone named is the *smaragdus* or brilliant green emerald. The fourth was a garnet or ruby, the fifth a lapis lazuli, the sixth, an onyx, the seventh was brown agate, the eighth, banded agate, the ninth, amethyst, the tenth was yellow jasper, the eleventh was green malachite, and the twelfth was green jasper or jade.

Most of the gemstones used in the breast piece of the high priest are also named as the foundation stones of The New Jerusalem in the Book of Revelation:

Figure 70. The title page of a sixteenth-century treatise about precious stones showing the high priest with the *saharon* or crescent on his headdress and the names and tribes of the twelve gemstones on the breast piece.

> *Her light was like a jasper stone, clear as crystal . . . the city was pure gold*
> *. . . the foundation was jasper, sapphire, chalcedony, emerald, sardonyx,*

sardiuus, chrysolite, beryl, topaz, chrysoprasus, jacinth and amethyst. (Revelation 21:9–21)

Isaiah describes the foundation stones of the New Jerusalem:

I will build you with stones of turquoise, your foundations with sapphires. I will make your battlements of rubies, your gates of carbuncles, and all your walls of precious stones. (54:11–13)

The throne of heaven is also described in terms of gemstones:

. . . there was a rainbow around the throne, in sight like an emerald. (Revelation 4:2–3)

Ezekiel describing his heavenly vision says:

Above the expanse over their heads was what looked like a throne of sapphire. (1:26)

The prologue to the *Zohar,* or *Book of Splendor,* of the Kabbalists tells this story of the old and wise Reb Rehumai who lived on the shores of the Kinneret saying to Reb Phineas:

Verily I have heard that our colleague Yohai possesses a precious jewel. I did look at that jewel, and it flashed like the radiance of the sun when he emerges from his sheath, and flooded the world with a light which radiated from heaven to earth and spread to the whole world, until the Ancient of Days was duly enthroned. That light is wholly contained in thy household, and from that light there emanates a tiny and tenuous ray which is shed abroad and illumines the whole world . . .

He said, "Go forth my son, go forth and try to find that gem which illumines the world. For the hour is propitious, Reb Phineas took his leave and embarked in a boat in the company of two other men. He noticed two birds which were flying to and fro over the sea, and cried to them, saying, "Birds, birds, ye that fly to and fro over the sea, go your way, and bring me the answer." Before Reb Phineas left the boat the birds returned with a written note saying that the son of Yohai, Reb Simeon was the jewel. When Reb Phineas arrived at the cave of Reb Simeon and his son Eleazer, Reb Simeon said, "Happy is my portion that you see me thus, otherwise I would not be what I am". He then opened his discourse on the precepts of the Torah, saying, "The precepts of the Torah which the Holy One has given us are all laid down in the first chapter of Genesis:

In the beginning God created . . .

While gemstones have always had a magical, heavenly quality, they have also, perhaps because of their extraordinary divine beauty, aroused the desires of men. A Persian legend says that when God created the world he made no useless things such as gold and silver and precious gems, but Satan saw that Eve loved the beautifully colored flowers of the Garden of Eden. Therefore, after the Fall, Satan imitated the colors of the flowers and made all the many colored precious gemstones to tempt human beings and arouse their passions.

Satan seems to have accomplished his nefarious purpose. Throughout history people have confused possession of magic jewels and precious metals

Figure 71. Turquoise stones. Blue stones are used throughout the Middle East as protection against the evil eye.

with possession of the divine spirit inherent in the gems, instead of seeking the divine sparks of the jewel within. Thus the prophet Isaiah warns:

The women of Zion are haughty walking along with outstretched necks, flirting with their eyes, tripping along with mincing steps, with ornaments jingling on their ankles . . . (3:16–17)

In that day the Lord will snatch away their finery and tinkling ornaments, and the headbands of crescent moons, the earrings, and bracelets, and veils, and the headdresses, and ankle chains, and sashes, the perfume bottles, and charms, the signet rings and nose rings . . . (3:18–24)

Instead of fragrance there will be stench: instead of a sash there will be a rope; instead of well dressed hair, baldness . . .

Figure 72. This Saudi woman is protected by her crescents, bells, blue beads, coral, amber, and turquoise. Her silver beads are decorated with granulations—or dots of silver that form disappearing triangles—which make evil flee like the abracadabra formula shown in figure 61.

Figure 73. A necklace of silver and coral. Coral and other red stones and beads are traditionally used as protection against Lilith, for fertility, and for good health. Red stones are good for the blood. This prayer case with coral and silver beads, bells, and *hamsas* was bought from Ruth Dayan director of Maskit and wife of Moshe Dayan on July 6, 1967, just after the Six Day War. The necklace was given to the author by her husband to celebrate the birth of their daughter on July 2, 1967. (Photograph by Junenoire.)

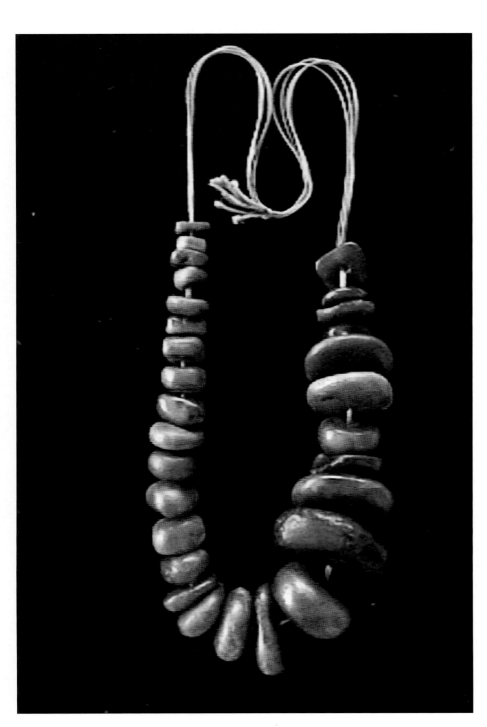

Figure 74. Amber beads with a particularly warm soothing feeling. Amber has traditionally been held to have healing properties. If you rub it the static electricity will draw bits of paper. The magic of the electricity is said to draw pain and illness away from a suffering person.

The headband with a crescent moon on it or *saharon* is none other than the symbol of the moon Goddess Ishtar. The tinkling ornaments that the women wore on their ankles were the same as the bells that adorned the hem of the high priest's robe. Similarly, these same tinkling bells are seen on the prayer case in figure 73 on page 120. It is sometimes thought that the plate of pure gold on the high priest's headdress in figure 70 on page 115 had the shape of the crescent moon. These amulets, talismans, and magical jewelry are symbolic representations of the power of the unseen almighty. They are symbols of the divine that human beings attach to an idea of God. They are used even today because people need a concrete connection to the unseen ever-present almighty God.

MAGIC CIRCLES

Like the triangle, the circle has a natural symbolic meaning in the realm of amulets, talismans, and sympathetic magic. The rather mysterious golden disk amulet shown in figure 75 has on its front a man, a woman, a lion, and the rising sun. The actual picture of a human being on an amulet is unusual except on Persian amulets like the one seen below, and the lock amulet pictured earlier in figure 68 on page 110. Traditionally, the man and woman are lovers. They represent love and fertility, the lion is strength, the sun brings warmth, enlightenment, consciousness, growth, and development. The images are surrounded by letters and some words. *Shir*, or "song" is repeated several times. There is perhaps an encoded verse from the Song of Songs, a song of both human and divine love.

The custom of the exchange of gifts between bride and groom when they form a loving connection, or are betrothed or married has come down to us from ancient times. Traditionally, these magic circlets would have been part of a bride price that the groom and his family would pay to the bride and her family. The wedding jewelry belongs to the bride and remains with her even if she is divorced. The Yemenite wedding bracelets shown in figure 79 on page 126 carry the feeling of being held or bound, or committed to a relationship.

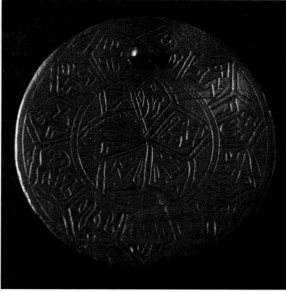

Figure 75. This magic circle amulet of gold used by Persian Jews has a picture of the sun rising, two lovers, and a lion on the front. This type of amulet is often given as a wedding gift. The meaning of the letters encircling both the back and front of the lovers' amulet remain a mystery. There are different formulas on the back and on the front of the amulet. (Photographs by Junenoire.)

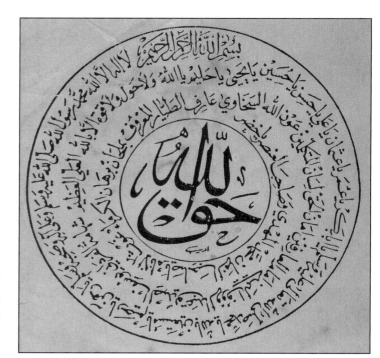

Figure 76. This is an amulet used by Naqshabandi Sufis. The form is a magic circle with the name Allah at the center, and prayers, Suras from the Holy Qur'an written around the circumference.

Figure 77. Shows Sheikh Hisham making the amulet in figure 76. It is folded into many triangles and wrapped seven times in Saran Wrap to protect it from water. Then it is placed in a leather or metal prayer case like the one shown below.

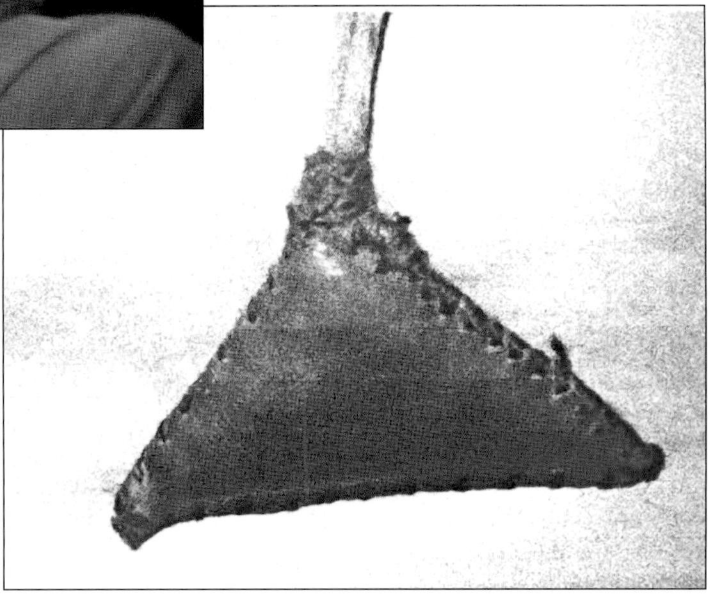

Figure 78. A triangular Islamic amulet case called a *hijaz*, meaning "veiled." This *hijaz* contains the paper Sufi amulet shown in figure 76.

Figure 79. Traditional Jewish Yemenite wedding bracelets are always given and worn in pairs. Often the silversmith who has made the bracelets leaves his mark inside.

Figure 80. Ring bearing the words: Strength . . . Completion . . . Healing . . . and the name of the person to be protected. (Photograph by Junenoire.)

Rings are another form of magic circle. They connect, and bind, and carry a powerful symbolic magic well beyond their size and weight.

Pliny relates a Greek myth of the origin of rings: Because Prometheus had stolen the fire of the Gods for man, he was doomed by Jupiter to be chained to a rock for eighty thousand years while a vulture fed upon his liver. Soon Jupiter relented, but to fulfill the spirit of the original judgment he declared that Prometheus should wear a link of his chain on one of his fingers as a ring. A fragment of the rock to which he had been chained was set in the ring so that symbolically at least, Prometheus was still bound to the rock.

Another myth about the origin of rings is that they began as knots. Rings made from a knotted cord or wire twisted into a knot were a favorite charm in primitive times. These rings or knots could be used to bind someone with a spell and deprive them of the use of their limbs or faculties. These magic rings could also be used as a protective amulet to cause lameness or disease to evil spirits.

Rings are often used as carriers of an amulet or prayer. The ring seen in figure 80 has the words *koach*, *shelem*, and *asah*—"strength," "completion," and "healing"—on it. It was found, synchronistically, by a woman at a time when she was in need of exactly these qualities and processes. The woman did not read Hebrew but was, nevertheless, attracted to the ring by its shape and color. The binding, calling out quality of the ring is obvious to others as well, but that may be because they too, are in need of its healing prayer.

Signs and Rings

The signet ring was probably a later modification of the cylindrical seal that was worn on a string or thong around the neck or arm in earlier times. It magically carries the name or identity or authority of an office. Rings can bind person to an identity or to a role. After Joseph interpreted Pharaoh's dream,

> *Pharaoh said to Joseph, "I hereby put you in charge of the whole land of Egypt." Then Pharaoh took his signet ring from his finger and put it on Joseph's finger . . .* (Genesis 41:41–43)

The custom of rings as signs or signets is mentioned often in the Old Testament. When Tamar, a childless widow, despairs of her father-in-law Judah ever providing her with another of his sons to give her a child as he was bound to do by law, she dresses as a prostitute and sits by the side of the road and seduces Judah. She extracts from him his seal and its cord as a pledge for a young goat, which he promises to send her in payment for her sexual favors. Later she proves that Judah is the father of her twin sons by producing the seal and its cord. One cannot tell from the Bible whether the seal was a ring or a cylinder, but it was, in either case, a powerful magical sign that not only saved Tamar's life, but in the end her possession of the seal gave her the babies she had so long desired. (Genesis 38:1–30)

There are many tales about the magical ring of King Solomon. With this ring, called the Seal of Solomon, he was able to succeed in all his endeavors. A rabbinical story tells how the ring was set with a magic stone—perhaps a diamond—so brilliant that it became a mirror. Solomon could see in it people and distant places, and moreover, he could make them do his bidding with the help of the ring. Sometimes the stone is called the *shamir,* the magic thing that engraved the names on the *ephod* and breast piece of the high priest. While in the possession of Solomon, it allowed him to cut the huge stones he used to build the temple in Jerusalem. The ring was stolen by djinns and lost by Solomon, but there are many stories telling how it was always returned magically to its owner, often in the belly of a fish.

The *Kebra Nagast*, or Holy Bible of the Ethiopians, tells that when Solomon and Sheba had lain together and she was with child and about to return to her own land, Solomon gave his signet ring to her. When her son Menelyk (whose name is derived from the Hebrew words meaning "son of the wise man") was thirteen, and about to visit his father's court in Jerusalem, he asked his mother, "How will I know my father?" Sheba held up a mirror to her son's face. "And how will he know me?" the boy asked. Sheba gave him the signet ring of Solomon.

Rings are used for betrothal and marriage partly because of their binding and connecting qualities, and partly because they are magic circles. The Hebrew word for "peace"—*shalom*—and the word for "completion"—*shalem*—have the same root letters: *shem, lamed,* and *mem.* The simple magic circle of a ring carries this feeling of love, connection, completion, and endless commitment.

Figure 81. Hebrew wedding ring surmounted by the Holy Temple, with doves and the symbol *chai* for long life at its base. The words *mazel tov,* for good luck, are incised on the shank. *Shaddai,* the magic name for God Almighty, is written on a blue enameled plate hidden in a secret inner compartment. (Photograph by Junenoire.)

A more spiritual connection to the religious communal meaning of marriage is seen in the Hebrew wedding rings, which have a temple surmounting the wide gold band. The Hebrew wedding rings with the temple and secret compartment were sometimes like the copy of the sixteenth-century Italian wedding ring seen above in figure 81, and sometimes, they were similar in design, but much larger and heavier and made of silver. These large ones were owned by communities and borrowed by couples to be used symbolically only during the wedding ceremony. All carry the legend *Mazel Tov*, or "Good Fortune," on the band.

Prayer Cases

A prayer case is like a dream. It contains the individual's dearest needs, wishes and fears. In many communities the word for the prayer case and the name for the prayer or amulet inside is the same. In Hebrew the amulet or the

Figure 82. Leather prayer case worn by Ethiopian Jews. The string also contains silver fertility charms from Ethiopia, amber beads for protection and healing, a coral bead for protection from Lilith, and an amazonite stone for good fortune.

Figure 83. Ethiopian Jewish magic prayers written on parchment and placed inside a leather prayer case.

Figure 84. An eighteenth-century Italian amulet prayer case with knives and praying hands. There is a small hole at the top so that a rolled-up prayer can be placed inside.

Figure 85. A prayer case that opens from the bottom so that a prayer can be placed inside it. It has *Shaddai*, the magic name for God Almighty, incised on it.

Figure 86. A Yemenite prayer case that opens on one end so that a parchment prayer scroll can be placed inside.

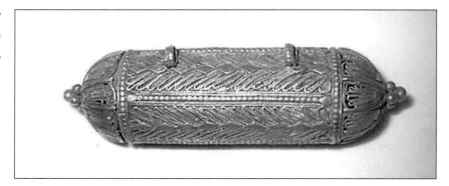

prayer case and the parchment prayer rolled up inside it might be called a *k'mea,* from the word meaning "fasten." The prayer case is fastened on the neck or arm of the person who carries it. The prayer itself is holy and must be protected by a leather or metal case. It is not to be taken into the cemetery or any unclean place, such as a bathroom—so warn the amulet makers and the rabbis. The amulet, if it is a tested and proven one, can be carried on the Sabbath, but it is not as holy as the Torah, which should be saved from fire while the amulet can be left to burn.

Yemenite women much prefer the amulet to be written on parchment rather than on metal. The written amulet and the prayer case itself are both called *kitab,* from the Hebrew word for "written." The prayer case is also called a *shamiro* or "guardian." The rolled up amulet is placed in the cylindrical type of prayer case shown in figures 86 and 73. Yemenite prayer cases are typically decorated with diamond- or flower-shaped pieces of metal. The number of motifs carries a magical Kabbalistic significance. Three, seven, and nine are the most important numbers. Often there are three loops at the bottom of the prayer case with three tiny bells or balls suspended from them.

CONCLUSION

Amulets, talismans, and magical jewelry most certainly "work." They have, as the rabbis decreed, been tested and proven. They work as a way of connecting people to the unseen, ever-present God. The glass amulets seen in figure 87 were attached to bottles of Bayer aspirin because even the aspirins did not work if the name of God was not invoked.

Figure 87. Glass amulets with prayers written on them that were placed on bottles of Bayer aspirin because people did not believe in the efficacy of the aspirins without the amulets.

Spirituality, Religion, and Mysticism

Moses Gaster has translated the directions given for writing an amulet. They are very similar to those given for writing a holy Torah scroll:

> The name of God must be written exactly as it is written on the scroll of the Law on specially prepared parchment. It must be written with square or "Ashuri" letters so that no letter shall touch the next. There must be a free margin around each letter. It must be written in purity and while fasting. It must be wrapped in leather or in some soft rag, and be wrapped round with a piece of clean leather. It is to be hung on the neck of the patient without his knowing it or when he is asleep, and he is not to look at it for the next twenty-four hours. The lines for the writing must be drawn on the hairy side of the parchment and the writing is to be done on the flesh side, and in the name of the patient. The parchment must be cut and the lines drawn in the patient's name. When the writer dips his pen into properly prepared ink he must say: "In the name of *Shaddai* who created heaven and earth. I, N, the son of N, write this *k'mea* for X, son of X, to heal him of every kind of fever." And then he must say the blessing of the *k'mea* as follows: "Blessed art Thou, O Lord our God, Who hast sanctified Thy great Name and hast revealed it to Thy pious ones, to show its great power and might in the language in which it is expressed, in the writing of it, and in the utterance of the mouth. Blessed art Thou O Lord, holy King, whose great Name be exalted.[4]

---

4. Gaster, Moses in J. Hastings, *Encylopaedia of Religion and Ethics,* twelve volumes (Edinburgh: Clark, 1930), p. 455.

These are the careful instructions given for writing a particular amulet. However, amulets seem to work even when they are engraved on metal, and when the eventual user is not the original person for whom the amulet was made, and when the person needs a particular kind of help not mentioned on the amulet.

There is a Hasidic story told of Rabbi Isaac, son of Rabbi Yechiel of Krakow. Rabbi Isaac dreamt three times that he must seek a treasure buried under the bridge in Prague that leads to the king's palace. When he had dreamt the dream for the third time, Rabbi Isaac set out for Prague to find the treasure. Because the bridge led to the palace of the king, there was a guardhouse at the entrance to the bridge, and so Rabbi Isaac was afraid to begin digging. Each day he returned to the bridge, and finally the captain of the guards asked him why he was there. Rabbi Isaac told him about his dream, which had brought him to Prague from so far away. The captain laughed and said, "And to please the dream, you poor fellow, you wore out your shoes to come here. Why, if I had had faith in dreams, I should have had to get going once when a dream told me to go to Krakow and dig up a treasure from under the stove of a Jew called Isaac, Isaac son of Yechiel." So Rabbi Isaac bowed, and returned home and dug up the treasure from under his stove, and built the house of prayer called the Reb Isaac Reb Yechiel's Shul.

An amulet or talisman works because, like a dream, it gives us access to what is right under our feet. If we can turn inward in prayer or meditation, focus on what we need, and call upon the angelic messengers and the sparks of the divine within, and do the all important digging, we can often get what we need. The amulet or talisman or magical jewelry merely serves as a template for this process. It is something to hold on to, or something to hang on oneself, or something to hang one's hopes on.

Yemenite Jewish amulets are usually inscribed on parchment. Often the inscriptions are washed off in water or vinegar and the resulting inky fluid is swallowed. The washed parchment is then rolled and placed in a silver prayercase, and tied or hung around the neck where it comes to rest between the breasts and over the heart. We need to focus on what is needed, and to articulate it, and then, to take the feelings of longing and fear and need inside ourselves, to swallow and digest and assimilate. Herein lies the real meaning of using amulets as a way of ascent to the unseen, ever-present almighty within.

The following texts and translations of the Old Testament I used were invaluable:

A Hebrew and English Lexicon of the Old Testament. Francis Brown, S.R. Driver, and Charles A. Briggs. Oxford: Clarendon Press, 1906.

The NIV Interlinear Hebrew-English Old Testament. John R. Kohlenberger III. Grand Rapids, MI: Zondervan, 1987.

The classical sources about Hebrew amulets and magic are:

Ma'aseh Book. Volumes I and II. Moses Gaster. Philadelphia: The Jewish Publication Society of America, 1934.

Sefer Yetzirah. Oldest of the Kabbalistic books, thought to have been written about A.D. 600. Aryeh Kaplan, trans. York Beach, ME: Samuel Weiser, 1997 (Revised Edition).

Sefer Raziel. Rabbi Eleazer of Worms (1176–1238). Written in 1230, Published in Amsterdam, 1701. My copy published in Hebrew in Jerusalem.

Sefer Zohar or The Book of Splendour. Said to have been written by Rabbi Simeon bar Yohai in Safed in Aramaic and channeled to Moses de

Cordoba in the fourteenth century. My copy Harry Sperling and Maurice Simon, trans. New York: Rebecca Bennet Publications, n.d.

The clearest exposition of the power of letters and names is made in:

Lessons in Tanya. Volume III. Rabbi Schneur Zalman. Brooklyn: Kehot Publication Society, 1991.

The classical research studies are:

Gaster, Moses in J. Hastings. *Encylopaedia of Religion and Ethics*. Twelve Volumes. Edinburgh: Clark, 1930.

———. *Studies and Texts*. Three Volumes. London: Maggs, 1925–1928.

———. *The Sword of Moses*. London,1896.

Ginzberg, Louis. *The Legends of the Jews*. Seven Volumes. Philadelphia: Jewish Publication Society, 1968.

Gollancz, Sir Hermann. *The Book of Protection*. London,1912.

Montgomery, James A. *Aramaic Incantation Texts From Nippur*. Philadelphia, 1934.

Schrire, T. *Hebrew Amulets*. London: Routledge & Kegan Paul, 1996.

Trachtenberg, Joshua. *Jewish Magic and Superstition*. Philadelphia: Meridian Books and The Jewish Publication Society, 1961.

General works about amulets, talisman and magical jewelry are:

Budge, E.A. Wallis. *Amulets and Superstitions*. New York: Dover Publications, 1978; London: Oxford University Press, 1930.

Kunz, George Frederick. *The Curious Lore of Precious Stones*. New York: Dover Publications, 1971; Philadelphia: J.B. Lippincott Company, 1913.

———. *Rings for the Finger*. New York: Dover Publications, 1973; Philadelphia: J.B. Lippincott Company, 1917.

Thomas, William, and Kate Pavitt. *The Book of Talismans, Amulets and Zodiacal Gems*. London: Rider and Company, 1914.

Figure 88. The author on amulet quest, Morocco, 1961.

Dr. Barbara Black Koltuv is a clinical psychologist and a Jungian analyst in private practice. She is a graduate of the C.G. Jung Institute in New York. After receiving her Ph.D. degree from Columbia University, Dr. Koltuv graduated from the New York University Post Doctoral Program in Psychoanalysis where she studied with classical Freudian analysts, Neo-Freudians, Sullivanians, Existential analysts and others. There she studied dream work intensively with Erich Fromm. Dr. Koltuv is currently a founding member of the new Jungian Psychoanalytic Association where she is a training analyst, supervisor, faculty and board member.

Dr. Koltuv has studied Torah, Jewish mysticism, and biblical Hebrew for many years. She has been fascinated by, and has collected, amulets, talismans and magical jewelry since childhood.

Dr. Koltuv is the author of *The Book of Lilith*, *Weaving Woman*, *Solomon and Sheba: Individuation and Inner Marriage*, all published by Nicolas-Hays.